G000066163

DOMINICAN REPUBLIC

Compact Guide: Dominican Republic is the top quick-reference guide to this sunny destination. It tells you all you'll need to know about the attractions of one of the Caribbean's most delightful countries, including its history-soaked colonial buildings, its simple villages, its rugged hinterland and its stunning beaches.

This is one of 133 Compact Guides, combining the interests and enthusiasms of two of the world's best-known information providers: Insight Guides, whose innovative titles have set the standard for visual travel guides since 1970, and Discovery Channel, the world's premier source of nonfiction television programming.

APA PUBLICATIONS

Part of the Langenscheidt Publishing Group

Insight Compact Guide: Domincan Republic

Written by Monika Latzel and Jürgen Reiter
English version by David Ingram
Updated by Sarah Cameron
All photography by Wolfgang Rössig *except:* Catherine Karnow (27, 33/1, 35, 38/1, 58/2, 61/2, 101/1, 103/1, 104/2, 108); Martin Thomas (6, 7/1, 8, 9, 11/2, 15, 16, 17, 22/23, 24/1, 24/2, 28, 29/1, 30/1, 30/2, 33/2, 34, 41/2, 45/1, 45/2, 46/1, 46/2, 53/2, 61/1, 62, 63/1, 74, 75/1, 76, 77/1, 77/2, 78/2, 83/2, 85/2, 88, 89/2, 91/2, 93, 95/2, 97/2, 101/2, 105, 113); Glyn Genin (50/1); Phil Wood (30, 34); Courtesy Dominican Republic Tourist Board (35, 74); Courtesy Tom Conlin/Aquatic Adventures (12/2)
Cartographic Editor: Maria Donnelly
Design: Roger Williams
Picture Editor: Hilary Genin

Editorial Director: Brian Bell
Managing Editor: Tony Halliday

CONTACTING THE EDITORS: As every effort is made to provide accurate information in this publication, we would appreciate it if readers would call our attention to any errors and omissions by contacting:
Apa Publications, PO Box 7910, London SE1 1WE, England.
Fax: (44 20) 7403 0290; e-mail: insight@apaguide.co.uk

Information has been obtained from sources believed to be reliable, but its accuracy and completeness, and the opinions based thereon, are not guaranteed.

© 2005 APA Publications GmbH & Co. Verlag KG Singapore Branch, Singapore.
First Edition 1996. Second Edition 2002; updated 2005
Printed in Singapore by Insight Print Services (Pte) Ltd
Original edition © Polyglott-Verlag Dr Bolte KG, Munich

Distributed in the UK & Ireland by:
GeoCenter International Ltd
The Viables Centre, Harrow Way, Basingstoke,
Hampshire RG22 4BJ
Tel: (44 1256) 817 987, Fax: (44 1256) 817 988

Distributed in the United States by:
Langenscheidt Publishers, Inc.
36–36 33rd Street 4th Floor, Long Island City, NY 11106
Tel: (1 718) 784 0055, Fax: (1 718) 784 0640

Worldwide distribution enquiries:
APA Publications GmbH & Co. Verlag KG (Singapore Branch)
38 Joo Koon Road, Singapore 628990
Tel: (65) 6865 1600, Fax: (65) 6861 6438

www.insightguides.com

Introduction

Places

Culture

Travel Tips

▷ **Paraíso (p85)** The Dominican Republic's biggest attraction are its palm-fringed beaches. This one south of Barahona is hard to beat, but you can also head for the resorts of the southeast or along the Amber Coast.

△ **Pico Duarte (p76)** The highest mountain in the Caribbean crowns the spectacular Central Highlands.

▷**Salto de Jimenoa (p75)** A good head for heights is required when visiting this waterfall.

▽ **Museo del Hombre Dominicano (p47)** A fascinating account of the island's first inhabitants.

▷ **Las Terrenas (p60)** A perfect getaway on the Samaná peninsula – a beach paradise.

△ **Catedral Basílica Menor de Santa María (p27)** One of the historic gems of Santo Domingo.

▷ **Caves of La Caritas (p88)** The Taíno leader Enriquillo used these as a hiding place when the Spaniards landed.

△ **Fortress of San Felipe (p56)** Built in the 16th century to protect the north of the island from pirates and buccaneers.

▷**Tobacco museum and factory (p69)** Learn about history and production in the island's second city, Santiago.

▽ **La Isabela (p62)** Remains of the first Spanish settlement in the New World.

Sweet Paradise

Columbus came here in search of gold and silver, but he also found what most of today's visitors come for: sun, sand and sea. Around 2 million tourists a year visit the land once known to the Taíno Indians as *Aíti* ('mountainous country').

The *República Dominicana* has everything one could ever hope to find in a tropical paradise. It's warm and sunny all year round, the coast is lined with magnificent beaches and groves of palm trees, the interior contains luxuriant meadows, hilly landscapes, tobacco fields and sugar cane plantations, all framed against the unexpected backdrop of high mountains. The people are cheerful and friendly wherever you go. They have a great sense of colour and a particular love of music: alongside more traditional refrains, the *merengue (see page 104)*, with its accompanying dance, can be heard all over the island.

This state of around 9 million people, which shares the island of Hispaniola with the Republic of Haiti, has made great efforts over the past few years to fulfil the expectations of visitors from abroad. A construction boom has produced a series of hotels and holiday villages; the infrastructure has been improved; and the old part of the capital, Santo Domingo, was given a facelift in time for the 500th anniversary of Columbus's arrival in 1492, which makes strolling its old streets and exploring its rich colonial heritage a real pleasure. The only issue is whether the country's natural environment will be able to withstand the onslaught of mass tourism.

POSITION AND LANDSCAPE

Hispaniola is the second largest island after Cuba in the Greater Antilles, the part of the Caribbean island chain that was formed after the North and South American continental plates drifted apart around 140 million years ago. The island has an overall area of approximately 76,500sq km (29,500sq miles), of which 48,500sq km (18,700 sq miles) on the eastern side is taken up by the

Opposite: La Descubierta near Lake Enriquillo
Below: windsurfers at Cabarete beach
Bottom: heliconia

Growing wealth
The Cibao Valley has long held out the prospect of natural riches. It was here that the Spanish conquistadors hoped to find gold, and later plantations producing sugar and tobacco crops created the spectacular wealth of a handful of families based in Santiago de los Caballeros. Today, the area is still an important agricultural centre, famed for its cigars and rum. As sugar has become less important, there are newer crops destined for export such as tropical fruits and exotic flowers.

*Central Highlands
near Constanza*

Dominican Republic. The Republic itself has almost 1,600km (1,000 miles) of coastline, and is bordered to the north by the Atlantic Ocean, to the south by the Caribbean, and to the east by the 8,500-m (27,900-ft) deep Mona Passage.

The landscape of the Dominican Republic is especially magnificent. The mountain ranges and hills on the island run northwest to southeast, with lush green valleys between them. The mountains of the Cordillera Septentrional, or Northern Highlands, extend across the coastal zone between Puerto Plata and Nagua, with their foothills stretching as far as the Samaná Peninsula. Here the fertile Cibao Valley connects with two large rivers, the Río Yaque del Norte and the Río Yuna. The valley extends over 200km (120 miles), from Monte Cristi as far as Sánchez.

The centre of the island is dominated by the Cordillera Central, or Central Highlands, which reaches 3,087m (10,128ft) at Pico Duarte, the highest point in the West Indies. To the southwest are the San Juan Valley, the Sierra de Neiba, the Enriquillo Basin (44m/144ft *below* sea-level and thus the lowest point in the West Indies) and the Sierra de Baoruco. In the southeast, the plain of Santo Domingo extends along the coast from the capital to Punta Cana. Farther inland it is bordered by the Cordillera Oriental, or Eastern Highlands. Two important rivers have their source here: the Río Ozama and the Río Chavón.

CLIMATE AND WHEN TO GO

Since the island of Hispaniola lies on the edge of a tropical zone, the climate is generally warm and humid (70–90 percent humidity), and alternates between a rainy season in summer and a dry season in winter. Statistically speaking, the months with the most rainfall are May and August; the least rain falls in January and February.

The precipitation affects the various regions in different ways. Since the weather is significantly influenced by the northeastern and southeastern trade winds, the

eastern slopes of the Cordillera get quite a bit of rain, as do the Samaná Peninsula, the north coast, the region around San Cristóbal and the eastern slopes of the Sierra de Baoruco. Extremely dry regions sheltered from the winds include the region around Monte Cristi, the Enriquillo Basin and the southeastern part of the Republic, east of Higüey.

Although they are heavy, the showers are usually very short, and bright sunshine generally returns within a few hours.

As far as climate is concerned, there is no ideal time of year to visit the Dominican Republic because the weather is superb the whole year round. The July to November period does, however, bring hurricanes.

Daytime temperatures along the coast fluctuate between 80°F (27°C) and 90°F (32°C) all year long, and at night it hardly ever gets any colder than 68°F (20°C). The mountain regions are of course cooler; high in the Cordillera in January, temperatures can often fall below freezing point. Water temperatures fluctuate between 78°F (26°C) and 88°F (31°C).

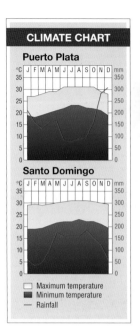

CLIMATE CHART

Puerto Plata

Santo Domingo

☐ Maximum temperature
■ Minimum temperature
— Rainfall

ADMINISTRATION

The Dominican Republic is composed of 29 provinces and the municipal district of Santo Domingo. The constitution of the Republic's

Palm trees at Punta Cana

representative democracy, promulgated in 1966, vests executive power in the president who is directly elected for a four-year term. Having occupied the post at the end of the dictator Trujillo's era, and again from 1966 to 1978, Dr Joaquin Balaguer managed a further three consecutive terms from 1986 until 1996. Dr Leonel Fernández Reyna served a single term as president, but was succeeded in 2000 by Hipólito Mejía. However, Dr Fernández was re-elected in 2004.

Below: the national flag
Bottom: guard at the
Pantéon Nacional

The constitution has been amended 29 times since it was first drawn up in 1844, and it places the president in a relatively strong position: he is commander-in-chief of the armed forces and also chief of police. Legislative power is vested in the bicameral Congress, comprising the Senate (30 members) and the Chamber of Deputies (130 members). Since 1994 voters have had four votes each: for the president, the members of the Chamber of Deputies, the members of the Senate, and the members of the district councils. The president also needs an absolute majority and may not be re-elected twice in a row.

POLITICS

Numerous parties were formed during the period following the Trujillo dictatorship (1930–61), and at the moment there are three principal ones. The the late President Balaguer's *Partido Reformista Social-Cristiano* (PRSC), is conservative. The social-democratic *Partido Revolucionario Dominicano* (PRD), founded in exile by Juan Bosch in 1939, was at the helm for six months in 1962 and again from 1978 to 1986. After a period out of office, marked by falling popularity and corruption scandals, the PRD returned to power in 2000. The party of President Leonel Fernández, the *Partido de la Liberación Dominicana* (PLD), was created in 1974 by Juan Bosch after he fell out with the PRD. Before its election success in 1996, it had attracted support primarily from intellectuals, workers and the poor. The PLD supports a more just distribution of income.

Democracy in the Dominican Republic began

tentatively in 1961, after the fall of the Trujillo regime, but the various parties, unions and political associations are not the sole source of power. The army, the Catholic church and the financial elite also exercise considerable influence whenever conflicts have to be settled.

THE ECONOMY

Tourism is the largest foreign exchange earner, with around 2 million visitors a year generating US$2 billion. Following a rapid expansion in the 1990s, the Dominican Republic has more hotel rooms than any other Caribbean island, of which around half are in all-inclusive hotels on the beach.

Traditional exports include sugar, coffee and cacao. Low world prices for sugar in the 1980s led farmers to diversify and land was turned over to other uses, such as golf courses. Non-traditional crops are expanding, with demand for tobacco and tropical fruit. Organic produce also sells well, particularly bananas and mangos, other products have been added for the European market.

Growth of the cigar industry has led to annual exports of around US$400 million, with the Dominican Republic competing with Cuba and Honduras as world leaders. The country's single largest export item, however, is ferronickel, from deposits near Bonao, which are estimated to be

Dubious polls

Elections in the Dominican Republic are usually heated affairs, and there have been many charges of cheating and vote-rigging since the return of parliamentary democracy in 1966. Joaquin Balaguer survived many such accusations as he won six elections between 1966 and 1994, but was forced to retire in 1996 amid growing pressure against another controversial victory. Hipólito Mejía's triumph in May 2000 was widely recognised as the first completely fair election in the country's history.

Below and bottom: coffee and coconuts, two important crops

El Dorado

Christopher Columbus came here in search of gold and silver ore – and it's still there, though the upper levels of the government-owned mine near Cotuí have been worked out and the costs of digging deeper are prohibitive. In 2001 the government started looking for private investors to begin gold mining again. There are rumours of large deposits near the Haitian border.

Below: flamingos
Bottom: humpback whale

10 percent of world reserves. Other mineral resources include gold, silver and zinc.

The Dominican Republic has struggled to gain financial stability for decades. Political leaders have traditionally borrowed money, spent heavily on grandiose projects and awarded government jobs to party supporters, while failing to deal with structural problems. The Mejía administration ended in failure and with financial scandals such as a banking crisis, the collapse of the peso, soaring inflation and severe electricity blackouts.

An agreement that took effect in 2005 saw the restructuring of the electricity system, the reform of the banking sector and financing of US$1 billion from the World Bank, the Inter-American Development Bank and the IMF. Public confidence rose when Fernández returned to office, GDP grew, inflation fell and the peso strengthened.

The key issues for the government today are fiscal deficit and the high level of public debt. Many people depend on the informal economy to survive and on remittances from relatives in the US.

THE ENVIRONMENT

Between its arid deserts and high mountains, the Dominican Republic has seven different vegetation levels and thus offers more variety than any other Caribbean island. Thousands of plant and animal species can be found here, none of which – apart from the American crocodile – is dangerous to man. There again, mosquito bites can be deadly if you contract malaria or dengue fever, and touching the giant millipedes *(milpiés)* which often live in houses can be very painful. But the small geckos scuttling around everywhere provide excellent protection against insects.

Along the coast, the coral reefs are home to an astonishing variety of fish, algae and crustaceans. The reefs, which are being threatened by thoughtless coral-collectors, also protect the bays from unwelcome intruders: sharks. The odd accident is reported, and because of this it's best not to swim in the more remote bays, especially where the water is deep. During the winter months, a fascinating spectacle can be observed north of the Samaná Peninsula: it's the mating and calving season of the humpback whale.

Protected sections of the coastline contain mangrove forests. The red mangroves are insensitive to salt water and have aerial roots, so they can survive even when the water level is very high. Black mangroves can be found in more shallow waters. Their roots are home to shrimps, small fish and shellfish and, because of this, flocks of birds nest in their branches: pelicans, herons, oystercatchers and frigate birds are the most common. Crocodiles are found near the mouth of the Yaque river and in the Enriquillo Basin. Turtles retreat to the more isolated beaches and river deltas to lay their eggs.

The coconut palms provide nourishment but also have a variety of other uses, which include providing material for domestic implements and building construction. The palm forests contain numerous species of birds such as the palm thrush, the *cotica* (the Dominican Republic's national bird, a small green parrot), and the Haitian parakeet.

In the island's interior, the handful of lakes are home to colonies of flamingos and iguanas. The dry areas in the southwest contain several species of snakes and scorpions. Their bites and stings are not life-threatening, but it's best to avoid the areas of dry bush and cactus they inhabit. Wherever

Below: coconut palm
Bottom: American crocodiles, native to the Yaque river and Enriquillo basin

more rain falls, there is dense evergreen forest containing exotic hardwoods such as mahogany, and also many rare species including the opossum shrew, or solenodon.

Below: a Dominican smile
Bottom: a new generation

A large proportion of the interior is planted with monocultures, especially bananas and sugar cane. Cabbage palms and the majestic 30-m (100-ft) high Royal palm can often be seen growing on these plantations. Areas that have so far been left untouched by agriculture contain large quantities of hibiscus, oleander, azalea, philodendron and the magnificent flame tree. The island also has more than 60 different kinds of orchids, with nearly 300 sub-species.

To protect the island's flora and fauna, nature reserves were created during the 1970s. Today, around 11 percent of the country is protected by 16 national parks, nine natural monuments and six scientific reserves, with a total of 67 protected areas. The rise in tourism is presenting problems, however, and for this reason only a few select companies offering excursions are allowed inside the park areas. The state-run firm Ecoturisa, for instance, operates cultural and scientific trips through regions of ecological interest. Travellers wishing to visit the parks and reserves should apply for a permit from the National Parks Administration (Dirección Nacional de Parques) in Santo Domingo *(see page 118),* or from the DNP office at each park.

POPULATION

The Dominican Republic has a population of almost 9 million, approximately half of whom live in the urban areas. As in most developing countries there are more young than old people. Thirty-eight percent are below the age of 15, while only 5 percent are older than 60. Eleven percent of Dominicans are black, 16 percent white, and 73 percent mulatto, i.e. of mixed European and African ancestry. Mulattos often refer to themselves as 'white' or 'dark Indians' *(indio claro, indio oscuro)*, even though the few Indians who lived on the island were almost completely exterminated by the Spanish a few decades after the arrival of Columbus.

This strange custom reveals an underlying identity problem in the Dominican Republic: although racial equality is firmly upheld, hardly anyone wants to be thought of as being descended from African slaves, let alone from anyone in impoverished Haiti next door, where the black population is more than 90 percent. Yet racial tensions in Dominican everyday life are rare, even though social status and skin colour do seem to go hand-in-hand: most of the top positions are in white hands. Spanish is the official language.

LOW EMPLOYMENT

About two-thirds of the population of the Dominican Republic live on the poverty level. This group comprises the unemployed (30 percent) and the 'under-employed', i.e. seasonal workers, street traders and tour guides, who make up another 25 percent.

The relatively small middle class is finding it increasingly difficult to maintain its standard of living. The monthly wage of a teacher in a state school amounts to less than the price of a night's stay in one of the better hotels. Many middle-class people are attempting to compensate for the rising cost of living by doing jobs on the side. The prosperous upper classes – mostly landowners, industrialists and merchants – account for just 5 percent of the total population.

Dominicans overseas
Over a million Dominicans live abroad, an estimated 1.3 million in the United States, where there is a large Dominican community in New York. Some are illegal migrants, but there is a well-established resident population in the US, many of whom were born there. Dominicans overseas are an important source of income for poor families, and an estimated US$2.7 billion was sent back to the country in 2004 by family members living and working abroad.

Bringing home the catch

EDUCATION

Six years of basic schooling are compulsory in the Dominican Republic. These are followed by four years of higher education which can be extended by two more years of practical training for a profession. Nevertheless, at around 20 percent, the illiteracy rate is relatively high, a situation which the government is trying to improve by building new schools, particularly in rural areas. Church-funded and private schools have a better reputation than state schools, though the high fees they charge make them a privilege of the few. Among the universities and polytechnics, the Universidad Autónoma de Santo Domingo claims to be the oldest university in the Americas.

UNLOVED NEIGHBOURS: THE HAITIANS

For decades the Dominican Republic has both officially and unofficially been trying to attract labour for the *zafra*, or sugar harvest, from its bitterly poor neighbour, Haiti – for despite chronic unemployment, it's rare for a Dominican to cut sugar cane.

You can see the Haitian workers on the country roads in the evening: shabbily-dressed black people carrying machetes. They've probably earned the equivalent of two or three US dollars for a 12-hour day, and are on their way back to the *bateyes*, their dismal lodgings without drink-

Old money

The country's traditional economic elite is made up of a handful of family groups – Cabral, Bermúdez, Vicini, Tavares – who have ruled the roost since colonial times. Mostly large landowners, these oligarchic families represent the Dominican Republic's 'old money', who tend to intermarry to keep their fortunes intact. They now face competition from the 'new money' of entrepreneurs involved in tourism and manufacturing.

The sugar harvest

ing water or electricity. Yet, many of the Haitian seasonal workers remain in the country afterwards.

As conditions have worsened in Haiti, the number of illegal immigrants to the Dominican Republic has increased; today upto a million Haitians are estimated to be living here. They are among the poorest in the population, doing jobs Dominicans consider either too dirty or too demeaning: cutting sugar cane, building roads or acting as messengers.

Carefree days

The Dominicans' attitude to the immigrants is ambivalent: on the one hand they need the labour, but on the other they're tempted to seal themselves off from Haiti completely. There are historical reasons for this: in the 19th century, Haitian troops overran the rest of the island on several occasions, and both halves of Hispaniola were ruled for 20 years by the Haitian president, Jean Pierre Boyer. Fear of infiltration survived into the 20th century: in 1937 the Dominican dictator Trujillo had 30,000 Haitians hacked to death in the border region.

VOODOO

Voodoo (also called *vodú*) is practised alongside Catholic rites in the Dominican Republic, particularly in the more rural areas. In Haiti it is the main religion, and is often celebrated in ecstatic rites, but in the Dominican Republic voodoo rituals are a lot quieter. People meet at the house of a medium, also known as a *servidor* (servant), in front of an altar covered with pictures of saints, herbs or pearls. As he dances to the sound of drums, the medium enters a trance-like state and asks the *seres* for help. These are partly African and partly Indian deities who can also be embodied in Christian saints. Possessed by the spirit, the medium makes prognostications or heals the sick with mysterious magic rituals. He is then showered with presents. After the ceremony there's usually a large feast.

Although it all sounds relatively harmless, voodoo has resulted in serious bloodshed. At the beginning of the 20th century, the faith healer Olivario Mateo (also known as Santo Liberio) lived in the town of Las Matas de Farfán, near San

Below: ancient Taíno sculpture
Bottom: Enriquillo, the warrior

Juan de la Maguana. His religion – a mixture of voodoo and Christianity – won him thousands of followers. He and many others were massacred in 1922, during a showdown with US troops.

In the 1960s the cult underwent a revival in Palma Sola (near Las Matas) when León and Delanoy Ventura, two Liberio priests, collected a large band of followers. Again, the fanaticism ended in bloodshed: on 28 December 1962 the priests and hundreds of their supporters were hacked to death by army troops.

THE TAINOS

Until the decade in which their fortunes were to change radically for the worse, the Taíno Indians had lived for 1,500 years in their little huts on the island they knew as *Aíti*. Members of the same linguistic group as the Arawak Indians, they had arrived on the island from the northern part of South America. In doing so they gradually forced out the Ciboneys, a stone-age tribe of hunter-gatherers. The Taínos still fought the odd battle with the warlike Caribs, but they were generally a peaceful people living off agriculture and fishing.

Tobacco was used ceremonially, and also smoked for pleasure in the form of cigars. The Taíno tribe revered its ancestors, and priests were the most senior members of the community. Spirits lived at various locations across the island, marked by wooden and stone statues.

It was in the fateful year of 1492 that three Spanish ships, the *Niña*, *Pinta* and *Santa María*, appeared on the horizon. Christopher Columbus had been commissioned by the Spanish crown to seek the sea passage to India. His men, a motley assortment of adventurers, had one ambition in common: to get very rich as quickly as possible.

Columbus's ships reached the north coast of the island on 6 December 1492, and on Christmas Day his men built the first Spanish settlement of the New World, La Navidad, near modern Cap-Haïtien. When Columbus returned on his second journey at the beginning of 1494 he found the settlement destroyed. All the inhabitants had been killed, or had died of disease. La Nueva Isabela was then founded, 100km (60 miles) further east.

SPANISH DOMINATION

The Spaniards made several expeditions into the island's interior in search of gold, robbing the Taínos of their treasures and setting them to work in mines. In 1503, the *encomienda* system was introduced: each Spanish settler was allowed to cultivate a piece of land for the Spanish crown, and the Taínos were promptly put to work. The Indians did not survive this sudden change in living conditions; many died from diseases imported from Europe, others took their own lives, or died at the hands of the gold-crazed conquistadores.

Some Taínos dared to resist the Spanish onslaught. The longest fight was waged by Guarocuya, baptised Enriquillo by the Spanish. For 14 years he fought his colonial lords until a peace treaty was signed between Spain and America in 1533. Today, Dominicans honour Enriquillo as a freedom-fighter, but his fight was in vain. Of the 300,000 or so Taínos who inhabited the island in 1492, only around 500 were alive 40 years later. At the suggestion of Bartolomé de las Casas, a Dominican priest, the Spanish decided to import slaves from Africa. Around 30,000 people were transported from West Africa to Hispaniola.

Ball game
A popular sport enjoyed by the Taínos involved bouncing a rubber ball with the buttocks and hips, with the aim of keeping it in the air as long as possible. This game was played in special ball courts, which doubled as dancing areas on ceremonial occasions.

Máximo Gómez y Báez, freedom fighter

HISTORICAL HIGHLIGHTS

c AD200 The Ciboneys are driven off the island by the Taínos *(see page 18)*.

6 December 1492 Christopher Columbus arrives on the island and names it La Isla Española. His first settlements in the north are destroyed by natives.

1496 The town of La Nueva Isabela is built on the east bank of the Río Ozama, but destroyed by a hurricane in 1502. The new town of Santo Domingo is founded on the west bank of the river.

From 1509 Under Columbus's eldest son Diego Colón, Santo Domingo flourishes as the first Spanish town in America.

1586 Sir Francis Drake pillages and partly destroys Santo Domingo.

1605–6 Governor Antonio de Osorio is ordered by Spain to resettle the inhabitants from the north and west of the island in the south, in an attempt to stop smuggling. The no-man's-land that remains in the north is settled by the French.

1620s Large quantities of gold and silver are discovered in Mexico and Peru, and La Española gradually loses its former importance. Many of the settlers leave.

1697 Spain cedes the western third of the island to France. The French colony of Saint-Domingue grows extremely prosperous from the boom in sugar cane, while the east of the island becomes increasingly impoverished.

1795 Spain is forced to surrender the eastern part of Hispaniola to France. Meanwhile, slave uprisings break out in the west of the island.

1801–4 Fired with the fervour of the French Revolution, followers of Toussaint L'Ouverture and Jean J. Dessalines plunder the eastern part of the island.

1804 Dessalines proclaims the independence of the French colony of Saint-Domingue; the first black republic in America calls itself Haiti.

1809 The eastern two-thirds of the island are returned to Spain.

1821–22 The colony declares its independence as the Dominican Republic, but is soon overrun by Haitian troops.

1838 During the Haitian occupation, writer Juan Pablo Duarte, soldier Ramón Mella and lawyer Francisco del Rosario Sánchez found the secret society known as La Trinitaria *(see page 44)*.

27 February 1844 Supporters of the Trinitaria, led by Mella and Sánchez, occupy the fortress of Santo Domingo and declare independence. This day is henceforth commemorated as the foundation of the Dominican Republic.

1861 Controversial president General Santana, who exiled the Trinitaria independence fighters, places the Dominican Republic under Spanish protection again, against the will of the inhabitants.

1863–5 Civil War (War of Restoration) breaks out and ends with the withdrawal of the Spanish and re-establishment of independence.

1882 Ulises Heureaux becomes president. He presides over a period of unprecedented stability and national growth, but borrows millions of US dollars in the process.

1899 President Heureaux is assassinated, leaving the country deep in debt.

1916–24 Having managed the country's customs affairs since 1905, the US occupies the Dominican Republic in accordance with the Monroe Doctrine. New roads, schools and communications facilities are built; the Americans also secure a large share of the island's raw materials and mineral resources.

1922 Massacre of voodoo faith healer Olivario Mateo and his followers by US troops.

1930–61 The dictator Trujillo (Rafael Leonidas Trujillo y Molina) comes to power and remains in control for three decades. Corruption flourishes and political opponents are tortured.

1937 An estimated 10,000 Haitian immigrants are slaughtered, prolonging the hatred between the two republics.

1961 Trujillo is assassinated on 30 May; his puppet president at that time is Joaquín Balaguer, who sets about eradicating his family's influence.

1962 Juan Bosch, leader of the Partido Revolucianario Dominicano (PRD), wins the first democratic presidential election. Seven months later he is forced to leave office after a military putsch led by Colonel Elias Wessín y Wessín.

1963 A military 'triumvirate' assumes power and appoints the civilian Donald Reid Cabral as president. This conservative government meets with massive popular resistance.

1965 With the help of a group of young colonels, the 'Constitutionalists', supporters of Juan Bosch, take control of Santo Domingo. US President Lyndon Johnson intervenes militarily.

1966 Trujillo puppet Joaquín Balaguer, at the head of the Partido Reformista Social Cristiano (PRSC), wins the presidential election. Strongly pro-American, Balaguer promotes foreign investment, wage freezes and an increase in exports.

1978 The social democratic PRD wins the elections under Antonio Guzmán. Guzmán commits suicide in 1982 after discovering that members of his family have been involved in corruption, but the party remains in power until 1986.

1986, 1990, 1994 The ageing Balaguer is elected president three more times, only narrowly defeating his rival in 1994.

1991 Balaguer orders the deportation of all illegal Haitian immigrants under the age of 16 and over 60. Negotiation of accord with the IMF leads to demonstrations and strikes.

1992 The Republic celebrates the 500th anniversary of Columbus's arrival on Hispaniola, in the face of protests at the 'glorification of colonialisation'.

1996 Presidential election won by Leonel Fernández Reyna of the PLD.

1998 Hurricane Georges devastates parts of the country; 200 people are killed in the Sabana Perdida shanty town. Damage exceeds US$1.2 billion and thousands are left homeless.

2000 Hipólito Mejía of the PRD becomes President with 50 percent of the votes. He promises an end to corruption and help for the country's poorest.

2002 Joaquín Balaguer dies.

2003 Hipólito Mejía's policies lead to financial scandals, bank collapse and widespread poverty.

2004 Leonel Fernández Reyna of the PLD sweeps back into power.

Map on page 26

*Preceding pages: the
Baoruco peninsula at Paraíso
Below: Columbus Memorial in
the Parque Colón
Bottom: activity on Avenida
Duarte*

1: Santo Domingo

The Oldest Town in the New World

No visitor to the Dominican Republic should miss Santo Domingo. Its cosmopolitan flair forms a delightful contrast to other, more provincial parts of the country. A visit to the capital also provides a complete picture of the island and its people. The sights here – especially the architecture – cannot be found in such a high concentration anywhere else on Hispaniola.

It's best to reserve two days for your visit to Santo Domingo, in order to get to know the Zona Colonial, or old town centre. After that, there's more to explore beyond the town walls in the 'Western New Town', and also in the east on the other side of the Río Ozama.

FAST-GROWING CITY

Santo Domingo covers an area of 162sq km (62sq miles). It has several universities, an international airport and is the industrial heart of the country. An increasing number of people are moving to the capital from rural areas, hoping to find work and a modest income. The fast-growing city has long since spread beyond its natural borders: the Río Haina to the west and the Río Ozama to the east. The city's expansion has caused severe

social problems. The gulf between rich and poor can be traced on the map. The villas of the wealthy are located in the northern suburbs. The city centre and the formerly prosperous residential area known as Gazcue are shared today by the middle classes; and the poorer sections of the community have been forced out to the edges. There are slums to the north along the banks of the Río Ozama, and along the main streets leading out of the city.

> **British vandalism**
> Sir Francis Drake's attack in 1586 almost finished off Santo Domingo. His men pillaged the town and burned large areas to the ground. Drake reportedly slung his hammock in the cathedral, which he used as a barracks, while his men methodically dismantled many of the city's finest buildings.

HISTORY

In 1496, Christopher Columbus's brother, Bartolomé Colón, founded the settlement of La Nueva Isabela on the eastern bank of the Río Ozama. The wooden buildings were destroyed by a hurricane shortly afterwards, and in 1502 the settlement was moved across the river and renamed Santo Domingo. Over the next few decades it flourished, becoming the seat of a viceroy and a bishop. When gold was discovered in Mexico and Peru in the 1620s, however, many Spaniards emigrated to the mainland.

Chess players in Calle de Conde

'CIUDAD TRUJILLO'

Until the 19th century the town's status continued to diminish; it was also severely damaged by a series of earthquakes. Its fortunes revived somewhat briefly after the Dominican Republic was founded in 1844, but it was under the dictator Trujillo, when Santo Domingo was re-christened 'Ciudad Trujillo', that construction work really began again in earnest.

From 1930 onwards new suburbs were built to the west of the old town, and the large *avenidas* and the Malecón (harbour promenade) were laid out. In 1961 the city had a population of 400,000 and covered a surface area of 62sq km (24sq miles). When President Balaguer came to power in 1966, more construction work began in the east.

Santo Domingo had 1.4 million inhabitants by 1981, 1.8 million by 1990, and today the figure has risen to 4 million. The daily power cuts, the

Map below

water supply problems and the polluted rivers illustrate the immense task facing the politicians in the coming years.

Dominican missionary Bartolomeu de las Casas

ZONA COLONIAL

It was on the west bank of the Río Ozama, at the point where the river flows into the Caribbean, that the chessboard-like centre of today's Santo Domingo was built in the first decades of the 16th century. In those days the Zona Colonial was the main Spanish base for forays into the American continent, and the magnificent religious and secular structures, many of which can justly be said to have been the first of their kind in the New World, date from this period. The ensuing centuries of stagnation here did have one positive

ZONA COLONIAL

0 — 300 yards
0 — 300 m

N

⑯ Iglesia Santa Bárbara
Calle Gabino Puello
Av. Duarte
Mella
Calle Vicente   C. Duarte ⑬
Museo de las Atarazanas Reales
Museo Mundo de Ambar
Calle Restauración
Alcázar de Colón
Plaza ⑫ España Tejera
Puerta de San Diego
Río Ozama
⑰ Convento San Francisco
Calle Emiliano
Casa del Cordón ⑭
⑪
Casa de la Moneda ⑮
Casas Reales ⑩
Hostal Nicolás de Ovando ⑦
Mercado Modelo ㉜
Hospital San Nicolás de Bari ⑱
Casa de los Jesuitas ⑨
Panteón Nacional ⑧
Iglesia Conventual de las Mercedes
㉚
Casa de Francia ⑥
San Lázaro ㉛
Old Town Hall
Parque Colón ②
Casa de Bastidas
⑲
Palacio de Borgella ①
Casa de Bastidas ⑤
Puerta del Conde ㉘
Catedral Basílica Menor de Santa María de la Encarnación
Torre del Homenaje ④
Parque Independencia
Iglesia del Carmen ㉙
Capilla de la Tercera Orden
Casa de Tostado ⑳
Santa Clara ③
Fortaleza Ozama
Convento de los Dominicos ㉒ ㉓
Colegio de Gorjón ㉑
Regina Angelorum ㉔
Puerta San José ㉕
Monumento a Montesino ㉖
Paseo Presidente Billini (Malecón)
CARIBBEAN SEA
La Hembra ㉗

result: the early colonial architecture is still largely intact. Even though the buildings suffered from pirate raids, invasions and natural catastrophes, they were never torn down and built over like their counterparts in the more prosperous colonial cities. As a result, the Zona Colonial is a splendid example of colonial architecture, ranging from churches and fortresses to ordinary homes.

In 1964, a group of architects decided on a restoration plan for the Zona Colonial, and President Balaguer made available the necessary funds. A second, larger wave of restoration began at the end of the 1980s when the Republic started its preparations for the 500th anniversary of Columbus's arrival.

ZONA COLONIAL (EASTERN PART)

This trip through the eastern part of the Zona Colonial contains numerous architectural firsts in a very small area: it begins with the first ever cathedral in America, leads along the first ever cobbled street, the Calle Las Damas, to the seat of the Spanish court, the Alcázar de Colón, and ends in the Calle Hostos, beside what remains of the first hospital. For quick walkers, the tour can be done in a day; more time is needed, however, if the collections in the Museo de las Casas Reales or in the Alcázar are to be properly appreciated.

SANTO DOMINGO CATHEDRAL

Begin the tour at the **Parque Colón** with the bronze-and-granite Columbus Memorial at its centre, erected in 1887 during the dictatorship of Ulises Heureaux (1885–9). The four ships' hulls at the corners of the base symbolise the four voyages of Christopher Columbus. The southern side of the square is dominated by the ★★ **Catedral Basílica Menor de Santa María, Primada de América ❶**. In 1521 the first bishop, an Italian named Geraldini, laid the foundation-stone after he had written a letter to Emperor Charles V complaining that 'as a bishop he had no roof over his head'. The majestic structure was

Star Attraction
● **The Cathedral**

Cathedral repairs
The 1992 Columbus quincentenary added impetus to the restoration of the Catedral Basílica Menor de Santa María, Primada de América. A chapel was dedicated to Pope John Paul II, who visited Santo Domingo for the commemoration, and gargoyles and sculptural details were added, depicting the Taíno people who inhabited the island when Columbus arrived. Extensive repair work restored windows, the roof and some of the interior masonry to their original glory.

Famous street in the Zona Colonial

Map on page 26

Riddle of the tomb

Almost three centuries after Christopher Columbus died in Spain, his (alleged) last request was fulfilled: his remains were transferred to the cathedral in Santo Domingo. When Spain ceded Hispaniola to France in 1795, one of the coffins in the Columbus vault was hastily taken to Havana. It remained there until Cuban independence in 1898, when the Spaniards reclaimed Columbus and shifted him to the cathedral in Seville. But Dominicans are convinced there was a mix-up: they insist that Columbus' remains were left behind, and it was the coffin of his son, Luis Colón, that found its way to Seville. During renovation work on the city's cathedral in 1877, a coffin was discovered bearing an inscription that clearly refers to Columbus.

Santo Domingo Cathedral

completed in 1540, and in 1546 Pope Paul III raised it to the status of Cathedral of the New World. In 1877 a tomb was discovered which many believed was that of Christopher Columbus *(see panel, left)*; a number of archbishops and presidents also lie buried here. Simón Bolívar, an ancestor of the famous South American freedom fighter, is interred beneath the nave.

ATTRACTIVE EXTERIOR

The cathedral is a three-aisled late Gothic structure with a raised nave. It occupies an area of 3,000sq m (3,585sq yds) and is 54m (177ft) long, 23m (75ft) wide and 16m (52ft) high. The pressure of the vault is lessened by mighty flying buttresses clearly visible from outside. Over the centuries 14 chapels have been built.

The western facade is the most attractive. Ornate Plateresque sculpture adorns the twin-arched porch. Note the Habsburg double-headed eagle at the top of the column between the two arches. It dates back to Emperor Charles V (1500–50), who ruled an empire 'upon which the sun never set' at the time the church was built. The surfaces between the pillars and pilasters are adorned with frescoes of saints. At the end of the southern transept is the Puerta del Perdón, through which the clergy used to pass on the way back to their

homes. The cross outside the portal symbolised the right to political asylum for the persecuted. The church is entered today through its northern door. The battlements on the portal are a reminder that the cathedral was once surrounded by a fortified town wall.

Below: chapel painting
Bottom: interior vaulting

INSIDE THE CATHEDRAL

The generously-proportioned cathedral **interior** is impressive, with its round columns leading up to the mighty ribbed vault above. The polygonal presbytery, flooded with light, is most striking. The 14 chapels were added after the main structure was complete, and are artistically decorated.

The Capilla Santa Ana in the southeastern corner contains the tomb of the wealthy conquistador son and later bishop, Rodrigo de Bastidas *(see page 31)*. The Gothic window and Renaissance arch at the entrance to the chapel typify the mixture of styles in the church as a whole. The Capilla de Nuestra Señora de la Luz, on the north side, is where the presumed remains of Christopher Columbus were kept until 1992, when they were moved to the Faro a Colón. Spanish claims that Columbus' remains are in fact stored in Spain, have led to a series of DNA tests to determine the identity of bones in Seville and Santo Domingo *(see box on page 28)*.

The Capilla de los dos Leones, on the west side directly adjacent to the north entrance, contains the tomb of Bishop Geraldini, who built the church and who died in 1524. The monument shows his coat-of-arms above two stone lions, and a wooden crucifix bears an inscription recording the decision to build the church. The elaborate stonework in the Capilla de las Animas, on the left next to the apse, is a masterpiece of the Plateresque style.

OLDEST STREET

On the eastern side of the Parque Colón is the striking **Palacio de Borgella ❷**, built during the Haitian occupation in the first half of the 19th century. Walk south down the Calle Isabel la

Map
on page
26

Católica. On the corner of Calle Padre Billini is the church of **Santa Clara ❸**, which was built between 1552 and 1556. The interior of this single-aisled church – originally consecrated to Saint Anne – has a marvellous coffered ceiling and a gilded mahogany altar. The convent next door was the first on the island.

Continue eastwards along the Calle Padre Billini and turn left at the next corner. You are now standing in Santo Domingo's first ever street, the ★★ **Calle las Damas**, former haunt of María de Toledo's ladies-in-waiting (*see page 34*). Many of Santo Domingo's profane structures can still be admired here.

Below: veteran of the times in Calle las Damas
Bottom: Fortaleza Ozama, with the Torre del Homenaje

ANCIENT FORTRESS

The ★ **Fortaleza Ozama** (open Mon–Sat 9am–7pm, Sun 10am–3pm), at the mouth of the Río Ozama, is the oldest fortified structure in Santo Domingo. Built in the early 16th century, this complex of buildings was given its neoclassical entrance in 1787, during the reign of Charles III. The inner courtyard is dominated by the 20-m (65-ft) high **Torre del Homenaje ❹** ('Tower of Homage').

Rebellious Indians were imprisoned and tortured behind the 2-m (7-ft) thick walls here, and the tower was still in use as a prison during the

early days of the Republic. The uprising against Haitian occupation began here in 1844. Until 1924, all the nations that occupied Santo Domingo flew their flags from the top of this tower.

To the south of it is a flat 18th-century building with 3-m (10-ft) thick walls – the former arsenal, named after St Barbara, the patron saint of artillery gunners. Between the tower and the arsenal, sections of ruined wall can be made out on the side facing the river-bank. The water used to reach up to here at one stage, and it was from this location that any enemies arriving by sea would be attacked. The dictator, Trujillo, ordered a higher wall to be built around the Fortaleza area so that the buildings could not be made out from the river. Whether such an investment was sensible in the 20th century is questionable.

Star Attraction
● Calle las Damas

Cortés' home
The Casa de Francia, built in the early 16th century, was briefly home to the ruthless conquistador Hernán Cortés. He joined Diego Velázquez in the conquest of Cuba in 1511, and later persuaded Velázquez to give him the command of an expedition to Mexico. Cortés set sail for Mexico from Cuba in 1519.

MUSEO INFANTIL

Next to the fortifications is the Casa de Bastidas, now the ★**Museo Infantil ❺** (open Tues–Sun 8am–5pm, Sat 9am–6pm). The house is named after its first owner, Rodrigo de Bastidas, who was one of the most influential men on Hispaniola, and he also made a name for himself as a coloniser in several other countries of the New World, notably Colombia. His son was the bishop of Puerto Rico and of the town of Coro in Venezuela. The sheer size of the arcaded inner courtyard – one of the finest surviving from that time – reflects the importance of the Bastidas family.

Further north along the Calle las Damas, take a quick look to the left down the El Conde pedestrianised zone; the restaurants put their tables and chairs outside during the evenings so their patrons can dine in the open air with music and candlelight. Just beyond the El Conde is the **Casa de Francia ❻**, also known as the Casa de Cortés because the conquistador, Hernán Cortés, lived here before sailing to conquer Cuba and Mexico. The French embassy organises exhibitions and other cultural events here. The foyer contains a collection of interesting agricultural implements from a Cuban tobacco farm.

A shady path

Map
on page
26

Death with dishonour
'Generalísimo' Trujillo had hoped to join other Dominican heroes in the Panteón Nacional after his death, and even had a tomb installed in readiness. But the dictator's ambition was not fulfilled: after his assassination, his corpse was removed to the anonymity of Père Lachaise cemetery in Paris.

Pantéon Nacional

HOSTAL NICOLAS

The **Hostal Nicolás de Ovando** ❼ was built between 1510 and 1515 by Indians under the supervision of Nicolás de Ovando, governor of the island from 1502 to 1509. Now a luxurious hotel, the house with its lovely courtyards overlooking the river is probably much grander than it has ever been.

Integrated into the hotel complex is another private home from the early colonial era, that of the merchant Francisco Dávila. It even had its own fortifications, the ruins of which can still be seen above the river. The Capilla de los Remedios was once the private chapel of the Dávila house. Its main entrance (usually closed) is on the Calle las Damas. This is where the colony's inhabitants attended mass before the cathedral was built.

TOMBS OF 'IMMORTALS'

The building directly opposite the Ovando House was built as a Jesuit church between 1714 and 1745. Following the departure of the Jesuits from the island in 1767, the church became a tobacco warehouse and then a theatre, before Trujillo had it converted into the **Panteón Nacional** ❽ in the 1950s. Today it contains the mortal remains of the 'immortals of Dominican history'. The bronze candelabra was a present to Trujillo from the Spanish dictator Franco, and the wrought-iron doors inside the building, with their swastika motifs, are said by some guides to have come from German concentration camps.

CASAS REALES

At the corner of the Calle las Mercedes is the early 16th-century **Casa de los Jesuitas** ❾, which was acquired by the Jesuit Order in 1711. Several of the rooms today form part of the Museo de las Casas Reales *(see below)*.

On the opposite side of the street is the mighty facade of a massive complex of buildings, the **Casas Reales** ❿. The front section of these 'royal buildings', which were erected in the early part of the 16th century, was taken up by the royal court of justice (Audiencia Real) and the audit office; the rear section contained the governors' residence and the island's military administration. The only eye-catching feature on the eastward-facing main facade is the attractive Plateresque window above the entrance.

MAJOR MUSEUM

The Casas Reales had various uses over the centuries until the ★★ **Museo de las Casas Reales** (open daily 9am–5pm) moved here at the end of the 1970s. The museum is certainly one of the most important in the country, documenting economic, political, cultural and military life from the island's discovery and conquest to its independence from Spain in 1821. Two highlights are an almost completely preserved 18th-century pharmacy, and a weapons collection with exhibits from all over the world. Opposite the Casas Reales is a small sundial, installed here in 1753 on the orders of governor Francisco Rubio y Peñaranda, and placed slightly at an angle so that the governor and his men could see what time it was from their office windows.

Carry on walking northwards as far as the **Puerta de San Diego ⑪**, once the most important gate in the city (1578). The eroded remains

Star Attraction
● Museo de las Casas Reales

Below and bottom:
Museo de las Casas Reales

Map on page 26

of three coats-of-arms – those of Santo Domingo, Spain and the island of Hispaniola – can still be seen on its eastern facade.

THE ALCAZAR

The palace complex known as the ★★ **Alcázar de Colón** ⑫ (open daily 9am–5pm, Sun until 4pm) dates from around 1510, and the central section is lent particular emphasis by the two-story Renaissance arcaded facade, eclipsing the unadorned side sections. More than 1,000 Indians were forced to build this structure, for which apparently not a single nail was needed.

The Alcázar was the residence of the first viceroy of the New World, Columbus's son Diego Colón, who was married to Maria de Toledo. Descendants of the Colón family lived in this impressive building until 1577. Many of the works of art and items of furniture (not all of them original) and also the exquisitely decorated wooden ceiling *(bigas)* were presents from the Spanish government.

Palace reprieve
After its heyday in the early 16th century the Alcázar fell into disrepair, especially after Sir Francis Drake vandalised the building in 1586. It was abandoned in 1770, then temporarily used as a prison before its roof collapsed in the 1830s. The Alcázar narrowly escaped being demolished but instead was neglected until 1957, when Trujillo authorised restoration work.

LAS ATARAZANAS

In front of the Alcázar is the generously-proportioned **Plaza España**, appropriately nicknamed the *Plaza del Solazo* ('Sunburn Square') by the

Alcázar de Colón mural

locals, because of its lack of shade. The western side of the square marks the start of the ★★ **Atarazanas Quarter**. During the 16th century this is where the town's main warehouses were located, and some of the attractively restored houses have been converted into bars or souvenir shops. The smart brasserie **Pat'e Palo** and the chic **Museo de Jamón**, where dozens of hams hang from the ceiling, are popular with artists, intellectuals and tourists, alike.

Star Attractions
● **Alcázar de Colón**
● **Atarazanas Quarter**

Plaza España with the Alcázar de Colón

MARITIME TREASURES

Highlights inside the ★ **Museo de las Atarazanas Reales ⓭** (open daily 9am–5pm) include artefacts salvaged from four ships sunk off the Dominican coast, one of which was the three-masted *Nuestra Señora de la Concepción*. In 1641 this ship was separated from its Spain-bound 'silver fleet' by a severe hurricane, and it struck a reef. In its hold it was carrying silver which today would be worth around US$52 million. In 1687 William Phipps, an Englishman, discovered the wreck and part of the silver, but it was only in the 1970s that the remainder of the cargo could be salvaged.

The 17th-century brick-built Puerta de las Atarazanas lies on the bank of the Río Ozama. Its wedge-shaped front section, specially designed to ward off intruders, has earned this gate the nickname *la flecha* ('the arrow'). Beyond it is the **Plaza Arqueología la Ceiba**. Excavations here have revealed sections of the former harbour. Plaques provide information on which section of ruined wall belonged to which building. The square is named after the kapok tree *(ceiba)* to which Christopher Columbus is supposed to have tied his ship when he first arrived.

DUARTE MUSEUM

Walk back through the gate now and along the Calle Vicente Celestino Duarte as far as the Calle Isabel la Católica, then turn left. Juan Pablo Duarte, the founder of the Republic, was born at house No 308 on 26 January 1813. The **Juan Pablo Duarte Museum** here contains several of his personal documents and artefacts.

Two blocks farther on, turn down the Calle Emiliano Tejera. The first house on the left is the ★★**Casa del Cordón** ⑭, which according to the inscription is the 'oldest (European-built) stone structure in America'. The building is named after the magnificent stone cord on the portal decoration. It was restored in 1974 and is now a bank. The employees provide a visiting permit on request, allowing access to the rooms and the two inner courtyards. Diego Colón and Maria de Toledo stayed here while the Alcázar was being completed, and Sir Francis Drake also used it for accommodation when he pillaged Santo Domingo in 1586.

Renaissance man

The Casa de la Moneda's Plateresque portal is very striking: its central medallion depicts a young man in Renaissance dress – possibly an idealised Charles V, the emperor who granted the colony the right to mint its own coins.

IGLESIA SANTA BARBARA

Continue westwards along the Calle Emiliano Tejera as far as the next junction. Then walk about 50 metres (55 yards) down the Calle Arzobispo Meriño to the left, as far as house No 358, the **Casa de la Moneda** ⑮. This building dates from 1542 and is thought to have formed part of a mint.

This is a good place from which to make a quick detour. Go up the Calle Arzobispo Meriño and soon a small square comes into view. Located here in the former stonemasons' *(canteros)* quarter is the ★**Iglesia Santa Bárbara** ⑯. Built in 1578 and severely damaged 100 years later, this building has several Mudéjar features alongside its baroque elements. The right of the two unequal towers has a stone window with fertility symbols; the section of facade directly above the entrance is broken up by baroque ornamentation.

Inside, the Isabellian-style decoration – small pearl-like rows of stone balls – on the windows and arches is particularly striking. Juan Pablo Duarte, the founder of the Republic, was baptised in this church on 4 February 1813, and his father lies buried here. Behind the church, a flight of steps leads up to the remains of the 18th-century fortress of Santa Bárbara.

Casa del Cordón

CONVENTO SAN FRANCISCO

Back on the Calle Arzobispo Meriño, at the corner of the Calle Restauración, stands a colonial building housing the **Museo Mundo de Ambar** (open daily 8am–6pm, Sun until 1pm). Different types of amber are displayed in varying shades from yellow to red and even blue. There are also videos, slide shows and a hands-on corner for children.

A block further to the west the mighty ruin of the ★ **Convento San Francisco**  comes into view. This 16th-century Franciscan monastery originally consisted of three sections: the large church, the Capilla de la Tercera Orden (Chapel of the Third Order) and the monastery building itself, complete with cloister and cistern. A massive archway leads into what remains of the single-aisled monastery church. The entrance to the convent – a doorway decorated with Franciscan coats-of-arms and cords – has also survived. This is where the Taíno Guarocuya *(see page 19)* was brought up by the monks, and baptised 'Enriquillo'. In 1673 an earthquake severely damaged the monastery complex.

ANCIENT HOSPITAL

Above the intersection of Calle Hostos and Calle las Mercedes are the ruins of the **Hospital San Nicolás de Bari** , the first hospital in the New

Star Attraction
● **Casa del Cordón**

Below and bottom: Convento San Francisco

Map on page 26

Below: relaxing with a cigar
Bottom: Calle La Regina, the street of tailors

World. The foundation-stone was laid in 1503 by Governor Nicolás de Ovando, but the basilica-shaped building was not completed until 1551. Although the hospital, which could accommodate around 60 patients, was a masterpiece of Spanish colonial architecture and survived several earthquakes, parts of it became so dilapidated that they had to be torn down in 1909. Beside the high outer walls, brick arches, capitals, and foundation walls still survive from various ancillary buildings.

Continue straight on and turn left on the El Conde, to get back to the Parque Colón. The building with its striking-looking tower on the right-hand corner is the **Old Town Hall** ⓮. It dates from the end of the 16th century, but underwent some radical alterations at the beginning of the 20th century. It's known locally as *El Vivaque* ('Bivouac House'), because during the Haitian occupation the soldiers used to come here to receive their daily orders.

ZONA COLONIAL (WESTERN PART)

Around half a day should be reserved for this tour, which also begins at the Parque Colón. It leads through the magnificent Callejón Quarter south-west of the cathedral, where priests still live today just as they always have, and along the Malecón, Santo Domingo's harbour promenade, as far as

the Parque de la Independencia. After a coffee break you can stroll back through the El Conde pedestrian precinct, making a brief detour to the Mercado Modelo which, like the Avenida Duarte, is very much the centre of bustling daily life.

CASA DE TOSTADO

Walk southwards down the Calle Arzobispo Meriño as far as the **Plaza Padre Billini**, with its memorial to Father Javier Billini (1837–90), who is reputed to have discovered the urn containing Columbus's remains in the nearby cathedral in 1877. On the southern side of the square is the **Casa de Tostado ⑳**. It has an interesting Gothic double window above the main entrance, apparently the only surviving one of its kind in America. The building, which also has a magnificent inner courtyard, today houses the ★★ **Museo de la Familia Dominicana** (open Mon–Sat 8am–4pm); here a bedroom, kitchen and living room on two storeys depict what living conditions were like for wealthy Dominican families in the 19th century.

A little further up the Calle Arzobispo Meriño on the right is the Casa de Teatro, a house dating from the colonial era which was converted into a small theatre and an exhibition centre for local artists in 1974. At the end of the street is the **Colegio de Gorjón ㉑**, built by the rich sugar manufacturer Hernando de Gorjón between 1532 and 1537. A school, known as 'Santiago de la Paz y de Gorjón', was founded here by the Jesuits in the 17th century; today, the building houses a number of exhibitions.

OLDEST UNIVERSITY

The Calle Padre Billini opens out westwards into the Plaza Fray de las Casas, at the centre of which is a large memorial to the influential Dominican priest Bartolomé de las Casas *(see page 19)*. On the edge of the square stands the **Convento de los Dominicos ㉒**, probably founded in around 1510 and originally a seminary before it became a monastery in 1521. In 1538 Pope Paul III

> **Writer's home**
> The Casa de Tostado was built for Francisco de Tostado, a writer who arrived in 1502 with Nicolás de Ovando's fleet. His son, Francisco Tostado de la Peña, was also a writer, credited with composing the first sonnet written by a colonial poet. Tostado junior, who became the first professor at Santo Domingo's fledgling university, had the misfortune to be killed by a cannon ball fired by Drake's troops in 1586.

Convento de los Dominicanos

Map on page 26

Polemical priest
Bartolomé de las Casas (1470–1566), commemorated in the square named after him, was one of the first Europeans publicly to condemn the extermination of the Indians. He became a champion of the oppressed indigenous population, travelling through the Caribbean and South America and writing the polemical *A Short Account of the Destruction of the Indies* (1551).

Monumento a Montesinos

promoted the theological school here to the rank of university (the first in the New World), named 'Universidad de Santo Tomás de Aquino'. It later became the celebrated Universidad Autonóma de Santo Domingo (UASD).

The ★**monastery church** is definitely worth closer inspection. Enter it through the richly-ornamented portal in the west facade, with its fascinating mixture of late Gothic and baroque elements. This church was almost completely destroyed in the 17th century and then rebuilt in the 18th. Of the five chapels, the second on the right is of particular interest: the ★★ **Capilla del Rosario**, dating from 1649. Four Roman gods are depicted on the ceiling: Jupiter, representing spring, Mars summer, Mercury autumn and Saturn winter. They are accompanied by the 12 signs of the zodiac representing the months of the year. The wooden altar in the apse, with its Habsburg double eagle, is also very striking. To the right of the Gothic apse, a door leads to the partially preserved cloister. Outside, as you leave the church, the building directly opposite is the 18th-century **Capilla de la Tercera Orden ㉓**, today a community centre.

PARQUE DUARTE

The palm-shaded **Parque Duarte** is surrounded by a number of well-preserved houses dating from the early part of the 20th century. A memorial stands in honour of the founder of the Dominican Republic, Juan Pablo Duarte (1813–76). A few steps away to the west, on the corner of the Calle José de Reyes, is the former Franciscan church of **Regina Angelorum ㉔**, built between 1550 and 1650. A number of alterations have been made to the building down the years, but some sections, such as the eastern portal, are still original. Inside there are two magnificent baroque altars with silver decoration.

Now walk down the small cobbled lane called **Calle La Regina**. This was where the tailors used to live, and the houses are mostly one storey high. Part of the wall of the **Puerta San José ㉕** still survives, and is now decorated with cannon; it can be seen at the junction of the Calle 19 de Marzo and the Malecón.

On the opposite side of the street is the enormous **Monumento a Montesinos** , depicting the Dominican monk Fray Antón de Montesinos shouting his condemnation of the conquistadors' treatment of the Indians across the sea. He denounced the barbaric behaviour of the Spanish troops in a famous sermon in 1511, extracts from which can be read on a bronze plaque in the hall beneath the monument. From the second storey there's a good view of the old harbour and the promenade, but it's also hard to miss all the rubbish that is thoughtlessly thrown into the sea.

THE MALECON

The harbour promenade known as the ★★**Malecón** extends almost 12km (7½ miles) from the old harbour at the mouth of the Ozama in the east to the western city limits, where it turns into the Carretera Sánchez. The section of it nearest the city centre is lined with numerous hotels, cafés, restaurants and discos. In the evenings, during carnival time and at weekends, this long promenade is very lively, although there is plenty of action further east on the Avenida del Puerto on the west bank of the Ozama. The promenade

Star Attractions
● **Capilla del Rosario**
● **The Malecón**

Below and bottom: Malecón seafront and promenade

Map on page 26

fills up with flashy cars cruising along to the sound of merengue music on the radio.

THE WOMAN AND THE MAN

Below: La Hembra, Plaza Rubén Darío Bottom: Parque de la Independencia

On the **Plaza Rubén Darío** is an obelisk known as **La Hembra** ('The Woman') ❷. The column, shaped like two slightly parted legs, was built to mark the repayment of all foreign debts by Trujillo in 1947. **El Macho** ('The Man'), its counterpart, can be seen 1km (⅔ mile) further up the Malecón; this phallic column (1937) is meant to commemorate the city's name-change from Santo Domingo to 'Ciudad Trujillo' *(see page 25)*. The formerly drab concrete structure has been embellished by the artist Elsa Nuñes, who created colourful paintings of Dominican women, and the mural *Tres Hermanas Mirabal (see page 72)*. The Mirabal sisters were murdered on the orders of President Trujillo in the last years of his dictatorship, and they are now a symbol of liberty and women's rights. The ruins of the old San Gil fortifications can be seen below La Hembra.

Leave the Malecón and walk down the Calle Palo Hincado towards the city centre. A short distance beyond the remains of the former town wall is the **Puerta de la Misericordia**, where the uprising began in 1844. The Torreón de Santiago and the **Puerta del Conde** ❷ were also gates in the

former colonial wall. The latter's name is derived from Count (*conde*) de Peñalva, who defended Santo Domingo successfully against an English attack in 1655.

Today the Puerta del Conde functions as an entrance to the **Parque de la Independencia**. In the middle of this small park with its canals is the Altar de la Patria, guarded by armed soldiers in full uniform. The marble mausoleum (access only if decently dressed) contains the tombs of the three leaders of the 1844 independence movement: Duarte, Sánchez and Mella *(see page 44)*. A bronze wind rose in the park marks the point from which all distances from Santo Domingo are measured; known as *El Kilómetro Zero*, it has developed into a popular rendezvous point. At 5pm every day the flag-hoisting ceremony provides an interesting diversion.

> **Short changed**
> One sort of street trader you should definitely avoid around El Conde is the money-changer. Offering rates above the official peso-dollar exchange level, these young men will attempt to fleece the unwary tourist with a range of sleight-of-hand tricks. Or they may just run off with your money. As currency transactions outside official banks and hotels are illegal, you will have nobody to complain to.

EL CONDE

The pedestrianised zone in the ★ **Calle El Conde** is far more modest than magnificent, with its shops selling clothing and shoes, craftwork, hamburgers and ice cream. Apart from the odd turn-of-the-century facade in need of renovation, the street is lined by a series of very ugly concrete structures. However, the stores here contain a many items sought after in vain elsewhere on the island: video and photographic equipment, electrical goods, specialist books and stationery. Here, as everywhere else on the island, anyone who looks vaguely like a tourist is regularly addressed by shoeshine boys, hawkers, money-changers or cab drivers, all eager to make a deal. The trick is to refuse with a polite smile, unless of course you feel like haggling.

IGLESIA DEL CARMEN

To the right and left of El Conde there are two interesting churches, just a few minutes' walk away. The first is on the corner of Sánchez and Arzobispo Nouel: the **Iglesia del Carmen** ㉙, built in 1729. A small niche above its main

Calle El Conde

Map on page 26

entrance contains a delightful Madonna statue just 1m (3ft) high. Inside the church is a famous statue of Christ, which is carried through the streets during the procession on Good Friday.

REBEL HEADQUARTERS

Opposite the little church, on the **Plazoleta de los Trinitarios**, is house No 255; it was here that the *La Trinitaria* secret society was formed in 1838. By that time the country had spent 16 years under Haitian domination – ever since the Haitian president, Jean-Pierre Boyer, had sent his troops into the eastern part of Hispaniola and captured Santo Domingo. The Dominicans were unsure how to respond: some were in favour of an alliance with France, while others, such as the landowner Santana, wanted the country returned to Spain. But a group of young intellectuals had very different ideas. They met in secret in 1838, in the Calle Arzobispo Nouel, and laid plans for an independent republic.

Their chance came in 1844, after Boyer had been overthrown by Haitian rebels and replaced as president by Charles Herald. On 27 February, the Haitian-occupied fortress on the Río Ozama was successfully stormed by Dominican rebels and the Haitian troops ejected. The unscrupulous power-politician Santana became president of the Dominican Republic – and one of his first acts was to exile the popular rebel leaders.

La Trinitaria

The leaders of the secret society known as *La Trinitaria* were Juan Pablo Duarte, a law student, Ramón Mella, a young aristocrat, and Francisco del Rosario Sánchez. The secret society worked together with the Haitian underground movement known as *La Réforme*, who succeeded in deposing Jean-Pierre Boyer. Mella and Sánchez led the raid on the fortress on the Río Ozama; Duarte was not with them. He only returned from abroad in 1845, when he was given a hero's welcome as *Padre de la Patria*. The plan was to elect him president, but he refused, thus paving the way for the ambitious Santana.

Crafts at the Mercado Modelo

LAS MERCEDES

A short distance from the square, on the corner of the Calle Santomé, are the buildings belonging to the **Hospital Padre Billini**. The chapel there, the Capilla San Andrés (1710), contains a very ornate baroque altar with the painting *Cristo de San Andrés*.

North of the El Conde, visit the ★**Iglesia Convento de las Mercedes** ③⓪, on the corner of the Calle las Mercedes and the Calle José Reyes. This imposing-looking structure (1527–55) with its massive square tower was once part of a monastery belonging to the Mercedarian Order. The single-aisled church, which contains both Renaissance and baroque elements, can be entered through a side-door in the Calle las Mercedes. Highlights include a bishop's tomb dating from 1644, the fine painting of *Nuestra Señora de las Angustias* (1734) and, above all, the main altar with its silver decoration which dates from the 18th century. The painting of *Maria de las Mercedes* has also been highly revered ever since it inspired the Spanish poet Tirso de Molina, who lived in the monastery from 1616 to 1618.

MODEL MARKET

Continue a short distance westwards along the Calle las Mercedes, then uphill along the Calle Santomé to reach the small 17th-century church of **San Lázaro** ㉛. Lepers were looked after here centuries ago; today the complex is a Catholic centre. The Gothic chapel and the ornate baroque altar inside can both be visited on request.

The Calle Santomé connects at its northern end with the Avenida Mella. On the right is the ★★**Mercado Modelo** ㉜, a modern market building entered via a flight of steps. This isn't just a food market, it's also a good place to buy souvenirs and craft products. If you can raise your voice above all the shouting and merengue music,

Star Attraction
● **Mercado Modelo**

Below: Iglesia Convento de las Mercedes
Bottom: shoe shine time

Map
on pages
26 & 48–9

it's fun to try and haggle – though the prices here are higher than in other markets on the island that are less accustomed to tourists.

The ★ **Avenida Duarte** is full of shops. People crowd along its narrow sidewalks – made even more cramped by street stalls – to buy all there is to buy. There's one department store after another, and traffic almost always moves at a crawl. This is the very heart of colonial Santo Domingo. At the northern end of the avenue, where it meets the Avenida 27 de Febrero, are the bus and *guagua (see page 117)* stops connecting with the east and west of the city.

Below: Teatro Nacional
Bottom: Palacio Presidencial

THE WEST SIDE

The interesting destinations in the west side of the city are so far from the centre that they can hardly be reached on foot. It's best to take a taxi or one of the *públicos* (shared taxis) that travel from the north side of the Parque de la Independencia westwards, along the Avenida Bolívar. The route back is via the Avenida de la Independencia.

It is possible to visit the enormous and inspiring, coral pink **Palacio Presidencial** (tel: 809 695 8000 for tours), which lies at the intersection of the Avenida 30 de Marzo and the Avenida de México. Built as a showpiece by Trujillo in 1944–47, today it is the seat of

government. As such it is not always open to the public, but tours can be arranged in advance.

The entrance to the **Parque de la Cultura** is on the Avenida Máximo Goméz. The park was opened in 1966, and contains several museums, a library and a theatre. The first building that comes into view is the **Teatro Nacional**, where operas, ballets and plays are regularly performed. Beyond the theatre are three museums – allow at least half a day to explore them. The first one is the ★ **Galería del Arte Moderno** (open 10am–5pm, closed Mon), the only museum on the island to provide a comprehensive view of modern Dominican art. There are also several exhibitions of contemporary work from abroad.

HISTORICAL MUSEUMS

A few steps further on is the **Museo Nacional de la Historia y Geografía** (open 10am–5pm, closed Mon), which mainly documents recent history, especially the Trujillo era (1930–61). Exhibits include weapons, furniture and photographs. On the first floor, three rooms contain items documenting the Haitian invasion and occupation (1822–44).

Beyond the natural history museum is the ★★ **Museo del Hombre Dominicano** (open 10am–5pm, closed Mon), probably the most interesting of the museums in the park. The history and everyday life of the Indians is illustrated in detail, and juxtaposed with developments after the Spanish conquest. Display cases in the archaeological section show a Taíno village, Indian jewellery and domestic artefacts. The ethnological section is devoted to Spanish and African influences on culture and everyday life; there are several fascinating items of clothing, masks and photographs on display.

NATURAL HISTORY

On the right-hand side of the park is the enormous National Library, and beside it the **Museo de Historia Natural** (open 10am–5pm, closed Mon). It

Star Attraction
● Museo del Hombre Dominicano

Death of a dictator
The Museo Nacional de la Historia contains some fascinating insights into the life and violent demise of the dictator Trujillo. One exhibit displays the white face powder he used in an attempt to disguise his part-African ancestry, while a bullet-riddled car is a graphic reminder of his grisly assassination on 30 May 1961.

Taíno sculpture, Museo del Hombre Dominicano

Map below

In the Jardín Botánico

shows how the island was first formed, and gives a good introduction to its flora and fauna. On the third floor there's a small café with a view of the city and the sea.

The **Parque Infantil**, to the west of the Parque de la Cultura, is a good place to take the kids.

PARKS AND GARDENS

There are several cultural sights along the Malecón. East to west, these include the **Palacio de Bellas Artes**, on the corner of Independencia and Máximo Gómez, the second-largest theatre in the city after the Teatro Nacional; and also the **Centro de los Héroes**, on the corner of George Washington and Winston Churchill, which contains the mighty **Monumento de la Paz** (*see box, left*).

To the northwest is the **Parque Mirador del Sur**. It extends for more than 7km (4 miles) parallel to the coast, from the Avenida Winston

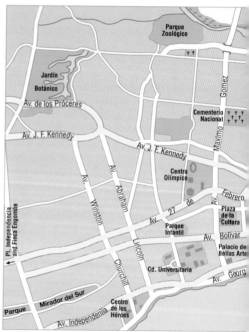

Churchill to the Avenida Luperón in the west. The park, which is intersected by a four-lane highway, was laid out in the 1970s and is a popular place of recreation for hikers, sports enthusiasts and weekend trippers. On Sundays, the wide Avenida de la Salud is closed to traffic, to make room for joggers, cyclists and skaters. There are several Indian caves in the park, one of which has been turned into the discotheque 'Guácara Taína'.

The ★★ **Jardin Botánico** (open 9am–6pm), which was opened in 1976, lies to the north of the Avenida J.F. Kennedy (entrance on Avenida Jardin Botánico) and covers an area of 180 hectares (450 acres). A visit here is a delightful experience, even for those who know nothing about things botanical. A tractor-drawn jitney will take the strain off aching feet and provide some shade from the sun, by transporting visitors past palm groves and all kinds of weird and exotic tropical vegetation, such as the national plant, the *caoba*, before arriving at a Japanese garden.

Star Attraction
● Jardin Botánico

Map on pages 48-9

Other worthwhile destinations include the Centro Olímpico (Avenida 27 de Febrero) which has a stadium and various arenas, and the delightful ★ **Orchid Park** with its 350 different types of orchid.

EAST OF THE RIO OZAMA

This tour starts off by taking you to the Villa Duarte quarter on the eastern bank of the Ozama, where Christopher Columbus's brother Bartolomé founded the settlement of La Nueva Isabela, then to the most monumental and also most recent structure in Santo Domingo, the Faro a Colón, and finally to the Los Tres Ojos caves. Because of the distances involved it's best either to travel by rental car or taxi – and you should allow four to five hours if you want to include the aquarium.

Below: orchid in the Orchid Park
Bottom: taxi driver

LA NUEVA ISABELA

Cross the Río Ozama via the Puente Mella, the southernmost of the four bridges leading to the eastern part of the city (the other three are the Puente Duarte, the Puente Sánchez and the Puente Juan Bosch). Then turn right down the Avenida España; the enormous 'Molinos Dominicanos' grain mill is a good way of getting your bearings.

The route to the site of **La Nueva Isabela**, the first settlement in the south of Hispaniola, leads directly across the factory grounds and through an iron gate.

The **Capilla del Rosario**, which is only of historical interest, has undergone substantial alteration. The chapel was first mentioned in 1544 when the priest, Bartolomé de las Casas, celebrated mass here for a missionary expedition to Guatemala. It reputedly stands on the site where Bartolomé Colón, founder of the city, prayed in an earlier, very provisional chapel made of wood and straw. In the mid-1980s, extensive excavations were carried out in this area, and although several interesting finds were made – including artefacts from the chapel and several skeletons – archaeological activity has ceased.

COLUMBUS LIGHTHOUSE

Continue southwards now down the Avenida España and turn left into the four-lane Avenida Argentina, which leads directly to the lighthouse memorial known as the ★★ **Faro a Colón**. This structure, as controversial as it is monumental, was described by President Balaguer, who commissioned it, as 'the eighth wonder of the world'. Several slum districts were razed to the ground to make room for the monument, which covers an area of 10,000sq m (12,000sq yds). The foundation stone was laid in 1986 and the Faro was completed in 1992.

On the outer walls there are plaques bearing the names of the different states of Latin America, and at night a cross-shaped laser beam could literally light up the clouds. However, the Dominican Republic's severe electricity shortages make this a very rare occurrence indeed (*see page 52*). A broad flight of steps leads from the west to the heart of the monument. Inside, the **marble tomb of Christopher Columbus** is guarded by uniformed sentries; his supposed remains were transferred here from the cathedral (*see page 28–9*) on 6 October 1992 when the Faro was officially opened. The rooms to the right and

Star Attraction
● **Faro a Colón**

America's tribute
The idea of a monument to Columbus is almost a century old. On 24 April 1923 the Fifth InterAmerican Conference in Santiago de Chile recommended a project representing 'collective feelings of gratitude, admiration and love for Christopher Columbus, the discoverer of America and benefactor of mankind' – and in 1929 the British architectural student J Cleave won the commission. The 'recumbent cross'-shaped concrete structure of the Faro a Colón is based on his original draft.

Faro a Colón

Map on pages 48–9

Map on pages 48–9

Map on pages 48–9

Controversial scheme
The Faro has been an object of controversy ever since its foundation-stone was laid; several bombs went off in the Zona Colonial on the day it was opened. Many object to the huge cost of such an extravaganza in a country where half the population lives below the poverty level. The 350,000-watt laser beams have not operated for years, because the city endures at least one power cut a day and many citizens have no electricity at all. Joaquín Balaguer defended his lighthouse project with the words: 'People need to wear shoes, but they also need to wear a tie. The lighthouse is that tie.'

Aquarium turtle

left of the long corridor beyond the tomb contain valuable colonial artefacts, documents and exhibition material covering 50 nations.

UNDERGROUND LAKES

Beyond the Faro a Colón is the **Parque Mirador del Este**, which was transformed for the Pan American Games hosted by the Dominican Republic in 2003. Unfortunately, most of the athletic stadiums and other sporting facilities built for the event remain largely unused. At the eastern end of the park, and best reached by car along the Avenida Las Americas, are the *cenotes*, or limestone sinkhole caves, known as ★ **Los Tres Ojos** ('The Three Eyes', open 9am–5pm). The 'eyes' are small subterranean lakes located inside this underground cave system, which can be entered via steep flights of steps cut into the rock. Vendors sell handicrafts outside.

After boarding a rope-guided raft and being taken across the second lake and through a limestone cavern you reach a fourth 'eye', another lake, surrounded by lush tropical vegetation. There are rumours that a crocodile has been living here ever since it was left behind by a French film crew. They had brought along three crocodiles from the Lago Enriquillo as extras, but one escaped, never to be caught again.

NATIONAL AQUARIUM

Those with time on their hands could drive another 2km (1 mile) along the Autopista Las Americas and turn west down the Avenida España at the next major junction. Along this avenue, beside the sea, is the ★ **Acuario Nacional** (open 9.30am–6pm, closed Mon), where all manner of underwater fauna and flora can be admired.

Turtles, sharks, rays and all kinds of colourful tropical fish swim about in this spacious and well-documented aquarium. One fascinating feature is the glass tunnel, where visitors can walk 'beneath the water' and see the fish from a seabed perspective.

2: Along the Amber Coast

Puerto Plata – Sosúa – Río San Juan – Sánchez – Samaná Peninsula (216km/134 miles)

Map on pages 54–5

Dominicans call their north coast the *Costa de Ambar* ('Amber Coast'), but that's only half true: the precious resin that flowed out of the pine trees here around 50 million years ago is today to be found inland, in the green hills between Puerto Plata and Santiago. The north coast does hold several other attractions, however, and each year it is visited by an increasing number of tourists from Europe, the US and Canada.

Visitors land by plane in the busy holiday centre of Puerto Plata, and can travel east to their hotels very quickly along the well-surfaced coast road. Sosúa is experiencing an unprecedented hotel construction boom, and its neighbouring resort of Cabarete has become an international windsurfers' paradise. The miles of white sandy beach on the way to Sánchez or along the palm-grove-covered Samaná Peninsula are the perfect backdrop for an unforgettable Caribbean holiday.

The tour from Puerto Plata to Samaná and back can be done in two days; anyone interested in taking a boat out from Samaná in winter to watch the humpback whales mating, or visiting the Los Haïtises National Park, should allow themselves a little more time.

Below: Glorieta Pavilion, Parque Central, Puerto Plata
Bottom: Laguna Gri Gri

Map below

Museo del Ambar Dominicano

PUERTO PLATA

Puerto Plata (pop. 85,000), capital of the province of the same name, is also the largest town on the Atlantic coast. It lies at the foot of the Pico Isabel de Torres *(see page 56)*. Puerto Plata was founded in 1502 by Governor Nicolás de Ovando, but later destroyed twice: once at the beginning of the 17th century on the orders of the government in Santo Domingo, who considered it a hotbed of smuggling and resettled the inhabitants in the south; and once again in a serious fire in 1863.

The attractive houses at the centre of the town, with their 'gingerbread'-style wooden decoration on the windows and doors, all date from the turn of the 20th century – which was when Puerto Plata became one of the island's most important harbours. But the town was almost completely ignored during the Trujillo era, and it was only with the advent of tourism in the 1960s onwards that prosperity gradually returned.

Puerto Plata is at its most architecturally charming around the Parque Central. The pretty La

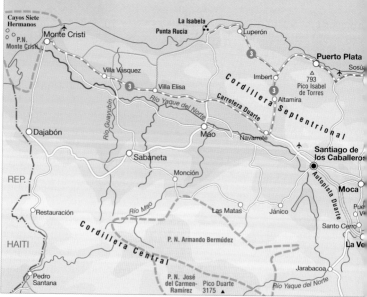

Glorieta pavilion at its heart was built according to a Belgian design in 1872. The southern side of the square is dominated by the church of San Felipe, constructed just a few decades ago; its matter-of-fact facade is reminiscent of art deco. The grid of streets surrounding the Parque Central – especially the Calle Beller and the western part of the Calle Duarte – contains numerous souvenir shops.

AMBER MUSEUM

At No 61 Calle Duarte, only a few minutes' walk away from the Parque Central, is the privately-run ★★ **Museo del Ambar Dominicano** (Amber Museum, open 9am–6pm, closed Sun).

On the ground floor several interesting items of amber jewellery and other souvenirs can be bought, but first visit the first floor, where there is a fascinating exhibition. The principal attraction here is a tiny lizard enclosed in amber. In 1977, an American professor is said to have offered US$25,000 for it.

Star Attraction
● **Museo del Ambar**

Proud Puerto Plata
Puerto Plata's golden age, reflected in its Victorian architecture, was during the late 19th century when the town was the centre of a thriving tobacco exporting industry. A prosperous class of merchants, some originating from Germany, dominated Puerto Plata's affairs, and encouraged civic pride with constructions such as the fire station and La Glorieta. The Amber Museum *(pictured left)* occupies the house of a former German merchant.

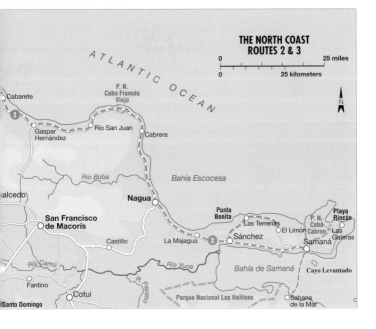

THE NORTH COAST ROUTES 2 & 3

Map on pages 54–5

Distiller's fortress

The San Felipe fortress has had a chequered history. The father of Dominican independence, Juan Pablo Duarte, was imprisoned here in 1844, and the building was again used as a jail during the Trujillo dictatorship. More recently, it served as headquarters for the Brugal rum distillery. Brugal rum is still distilled in Puerto Plata, and the bottling plant on Avenida Luis Ginebra can be visited for free samples and purchases.

SAN FELIPE FORTRESS

At the western end of the harbour promenade, the Avenida Gregorio Luperón, is the ★ **Fortress of San Felipe** (open daily 9am–5pm), the only visible reminder in Puerto Plata of the early colonial era. Built between 1564 and 1577, this bastion was meant to protect the north of the island from raids by pirates and buccaneers. Thanks to restoration work begun in 1973, the almost square fortress now looks very much the way it used to when it was first built: the eastern entrance flanked by two small towers, the massive keep at the centre, and the small look-out towers on the two corners of the wall facing the sea.

The room on the right as you enter the keep is a military museum; most of the exhibits date from the 18th century. On the left is a small photographic exhibition documenting the restoration work. Both these rooms have very low entrances, so remember to duck. The observation platform on top of the keep is also open to visitors: through the arrow slits you can see the harbour across to the west which the fortress was meant to protect.

MOUNTAIN VIEW

Fortress of San Felipe

Travel west, via the Avenida Circunvalación Sur to reach the Carretera 5, and as you leave Puerto Plata the impressive ★★ **Pico Isabel de Torres** (800m/2,600ft) comes into view on the left. A section of rain forest on this mountain is taken up by the Reserva Científica Natural Isabel de Torres, a nature reserve with up to 30 different species of protected birds. From the summit you will not only have a fantastic panoramic ★★ **view** but will also be able to see the 16-m (52-ft) statue of *Cristo Redentor* up close, buy souvenirs, eat lunch or stroll through a botanical garden.

There are three ways of reaching the top: on foot, which takes about two hours; by car along a rough road, which takes around 20 minutes; or you can take the cable car (*teleférico;* open 8.30am–5pm, closed Wed). The service can be suspended on windy days, and in peak season be prepared to wait for some time.

Puerto Plata has some fine beaches. The Long Beach is located at the eastern end of the harbour promenade, and just beyond it are the well-equipped beaches of the Playa Dorada hotel complex. Further east is the **Columbus Aquapark**. There are also several small beaches to the west of the town; to find them just follow the 'Costambar' signs. The **Playa Cofresí**, 7km (4 miles) out of town, is dominated by **Ocean World Adventure Park**, where dolphins captured from the wild have been trained to entertain tourists. It is currently the leading attraction on the north coast, with performing sea lions, sharks and sting rays completing the 'encounter' programme.

Star Attraction
● Pico Isabel de Torres and view

Below: Sosúa beach
Bottom: Pico Isabel de Torres from Puerto Plata

SOSUA

The town of **Sosúa** (pop. 11,000), 27km (17 miles) to the east of Puerto Plata, consists of two different sections separated by a kilometre-long sandy beach: the fishing village of Los Charamicos in the west, and the characteristically European quarter known as El Batey to the east of the horseshoe-shaped bay.

El Batey owes its existence to the racist policies of two dictators: Adolf Hitler and General Trujillo. Trujillo allowed Jewish refugees to settle here because he thought that an infusion of European blood would 'lighten' the skins of the

Map on pages 54–5

island's population. At the beginning of the 1940s around 600 Jewish immigrants (rather than the expected 100,000) settled in Sosúa, ploughed the land and very soon developed a flourishing dairy farming industry. Many of those settlers have now emigrated again, but several reminders of their stay survive, including memorial plaques, street-names, a synagogue and also a **Jewish Museum** (in the Calle Dr Alejo Martinez).

El Batey, especially the area around the Calle Pedro Clisante, contains everything a tourist would wish to find: restaurants, cafés, bars, discos, souvenir shops, and also travel firms organising trips. There are several thousand German immigrants living here and so the place has quite a German flavour to it: there's delicious German bread, and restaurants serve *schnitzel*. Mass tourism is making distinct inroads, however: the famed hospitality is becoming increasingly money-based, and quite a few young Dominican girls are turning to prostitution.

Below: synagogue, Sosúa
Bottom: windsurfer on Cabarete beach

CABARETE AND BEYOND

The road leads east to ★**Cabarete**, 39km (24 miles) from Puerto Plata and the Dominican Republic's windsurfing and kite surfing paradise. Cabarete's main street and its 2km- (1-mile-) long sandy beach is lined with dozens of hotels and

bungalow complexes, beach bars, restaurants, windsurfing and kite surfing schools.

The Carretera 5 leads you past miles of palm-lined beaches, and 90km (55 miles) further on arrives at the fishing town of **Río San Juan** (pop. 10,000). This is a day-trip destination, because nearby is the ★ **Laguna Gri Gri**, at the end of the main street, the Calle Duarte. Boats taking from 10 to 20 passengers set out from a pond-like stretch of water on a two-hour trip, along a canal lined with **mangrove trees** which leads to the open sea. The boats circle an area of coral and then chug along the coast, passing several caves, until they enter the largest one, filled with stalagmites and stalactites. A swim in a 'natural pool' *(piscina natural)* is the highlight of the return journey.

NATIONAL PARK

Almost 20km (12 miles) further along the coast road, a small road branches off to the tiny **Cabo Francés Viejo National Park**, a protected area of rain forest. A good place for a break is the **Playa Grande**, visible from the road; the locals living in the wooden huts on the beach make delicious seafood dishes. There are several all-inclusive hotels in this area and one of the world's most attractive golf courses. The lush area from Río San Juan around the coast to Cabrera is known as the Costa Verde.

SAMANA PENINSULA

Nagua (pop. 58,000) is 149km (93 miles) from Puerto Plata. Although it is the capital of the province of Maria Trinidad Sánchez, the town has little to offer visitors. On the left as you leave Nagua is the Parque de Recreo, with a statue of Maria Trinidad Sánchez, who sewed the first Dominican flag after the victory of 1844.

Near Majagua the road veers away from the sea and crosses a flat stretch of land at the foot of the ★★ **Samaná Peninsula**, which was separated from the mainland by a strait until the 18th century, but remains a tropical paradise.

Star Attraction
● **Samaná Peninsula**

International venue
Cabarete was a small, sleepy fishing village until the 1980s, when Canadian wind-surfers discovered its ideal combination of wind, waves and beach. The town is now internationally famous for windsurfing and has hosted the World Windsurf Championship. For the less courageous, it has also been the venue for the world sand-castle building competition.

Playa Grande

Map
on pages
54–5

End of the line

Sánchez's economic decline was hastened by Trujillo, who had the railway line torn up and removed for use in his own sugar plantations. With the railway gone, the town no longer served as a convenient point for exporting produce from the Cibao Valley and it fell into a state of irreversible disrepair.

House in Sánchez

LAS TERRENAS

The quiet town of **Sánchez** (pop. 22,000) was once an important harbour and also the terminus of the island's only railway line, which used to run to La Vega but has now closed. A row of attractive Victorian-style wooden houses still survives from that time.

Sánchez is a good place to make a detour to ★★ **Las Terrenas** (pop. 13,000), on the north coast of the peninsula. A well-surfaced road, rather steep in places, leads off to the left and across a delightful stretch of hilly landscape with luxuriant vegetation. It climbs to an altitude of 450m (1,476ft) before descending to sea-level again. Las Terrenas is a beach paradise offering absolutely everything: diving, windsurfing, bathing beaches, fish cooked in coconut milk and served right next to the sea, you name it. At the western end of the beach a footpath leads over a small rise to ★ **Playa Bonita** (15 minutes' walk), where there are several beach hotels (to drive there, turn left as you arrive in Las Terrenas).

East from Las Terrenas, 15km (9 miles) along a paved road, is the village of **El Limón**, where you can hire a guide to take you on a hike to the 50-m (164-ft) high El Limón waterfall.

SAMANA

After this detour, continue east along the Carretera 5 from Sánchez, through a rolling landscape filled with coconut groves and colourful houses. Around 20km (12 miles) from Sánchez, a road branches off to Arroyo Barril Airport, and 14km (8 miles) further on is the town of **Santa Bárbara de Samaná** (pop. 40,000), the capital of Samaná Province and usually known as Samaná for short.

It was close to this *Golfo de las Flechas* ('bay of arrows'), as Columbus called the bay, that settlers from the Canary Islands founded the community of Santa Bárbara in 1756 at the behest of Governor Rubio y Peñaranda. Numerous freed slaves from the US settled here, too, at the beginning of the 19th century. Their mainly Protestant descendants – named Smith, King or

Williams – make up the majority of the rural population. In 1946 there was a serious fire in the town, but the 19th-century Protestant church, La Churcha, survived virtually unscathed.

PARADISE BEACHES

On the whole, Samaná, with its broad harbour promenade, is not an idyllic place. But the beaches in the vicinity are Caribbean paradises, especially ★ **Cayo Levantado**. Water taxis and fishing boats make regular trips to this island, although hotel construction has marred the peace a bit. There are several tiny islands in the bay, some of which are connected by footbridges, others have a hotel. A good excursion destination by boat from Samaná is the ★★ **Los Haïtises National Park**; highlights include several species of rare birds, the opossum shrew, and also limestone caverns containing pre-Columbian wall paintings *(see page 100)*.

Another popular pastime off the coast of Samaná in the winter months is ★ **whale watching**. From mid-January to mid-March between 2,000 and 3,000 humpback whales come here from the north to mate and calve. Watching these gigantic creatures (that weigh up to 40 tons) rolling and diving is a majestic sight. Whale watching boats are strictly regulated and operators must follow rigid guidelines when approaching the whales.

Star Attractions
● **Las Terrenas**
● **Los Haïtises National Park**

Below: Cayo Levantado
Bottom: boating at
Las Terrenas

3: On the Trail of Christopher Columbus

Puerto Plata – Luperón/La Isabela – Navarrete – Punta Rucia – Monte Cristi (138km/85 miles)

Fine falls

Just west of the village of Imbert, after the turn to Luperón, are a series of 27 spectacular waterfalls, part of the Río Baja-bonica. It is possible to swim in some of the pools or climb the hill to be rewarded with a fine view. Ask in Imbert for directions.

Girl in Luperón

The western section of the Amber Coast couldn't be more of a contrast to the eastern one: travelling here you are more likely to meet a horse or mule coming the other way than a car. The arid region around Monte Cristi, close to the Haitian border, has scarcely been touched by international tourism. There's no single coast road, so the sights are often reached along extremely bumpy tracks.

But with the road there now surfaced, visitors will need only an hour to reach the area's principal attraction, namely the ruins of La Isabela, the settlement founded by Columbus more than 500 years ago.

LA ISABELA

Leave Puerto Plata *(see page 54)* along the Avenida Circunvalación Sur and the Carretera 5 in the direction of Santiago. The detour to Luperón and La Isabela begins 20km (12 miles) out of town, and the distance there and back is 88km (55 miles). Near Imbert, just before two large petrol stations with snack-stands, the Carretera 30 branches off to the right. The cactus hedges along the side of the road are used to mark real-estate boundaries.

Having travelled 25km (15 miles) along this route and successfully dodged more donkeys and mules than anything motorised, you will see **Luperón** come into view – a dusty, sleepy fishing village, with little to indicate the presence of the Luperón Beach Resort holiday village 5km (3 miles) away. A housing and marina development is underway, which will take advantage of the protected harbour among the mangroves.

Turn left off Luperón's long central square in the direction of **La Isabela**. The journey continues now along a track strewn with rubble, frequented by several herds of animals, for 15km (9 miles) as far as a T-junction, where you turn right. The route continues across a savanna-like landscape for around 4km (2½ miles), running partially parallel to the small Bajabonica river. At the end of it you'll see souvenir stands, a *comedor* (roadside restaurant) and a fenced-in area of red sand, the ★★ **Arqueología Parque Nacional Historico La Isabela** – all that remains of the first European settlement in the New World.

SPANISH REMAINS

When Christopher Columbus returned to Hispaniola on his second voyage (1493–6) he discovered that the settlement of La Navidad (in today's Haiti) had been destroyed and the 39 men he had left behind were all dead – either murdered by Indians or killed by disease. His little fleet made its way eastwards and on 1 January 1494 dropped anchor in a broad, idyllic bay. Here Columbus founded a settlement in honour of the Spanish queen: 'La Isabela'.

Excavation work, which began in the 1950s, was speeded up in 1992 in preparation for the 500th anniversary of the discovery of the New World. Stone walls today reconstruct the outlines of the main buildings, such as the church (15m/49ft by 5m/16ft) in which the first Mass on American soil was read on 6 January 1494. Some of Columbus's house has now fallen into

Below: the Templo de las Americas at the (bottom) Parque Arqueología Nacional Historico La Isabela

Map on pages 54–5

the sea through erosion; the semicircular tiles in the corner came from the building's first roof.

Wooden crosses beyond the church mark the site of the cemetery. Some of the tombs have been excavated; they contain the skeletons of victims of the *Conquista*. The Spanish dead can be recognised by their folded arms. Rebels and prisoners were buried with their hands tied, sometimes facing downwards; the Indians lie in embryonic postures. La Isabela was abandoned in 1498. Finds from the site include iron cannonballs, crucifixes, sections of chain-mail and dagger scabbards.

Near the excavation site is the colonial-style **Templo de las Americas** memorial church, where the Pope said Mass in 1992 during his visit to the Dominican Republic. The small road to the west of La Isabela, which leads either 16km (10 miles) further on to Punta Rucia or back again via Los Hidalgos to the Carretera Duarte, is not recommended: it crosses two streams which aren't always passable. It is best to follow the route described back to Imbert.

Eager to please

Legend has it that Trujillo once planned a visit to La Isabela and sent orders that the site should be cleared up in readiness for his arrival. Workers took his orders a little too literally and proceeded to bulldoze much of the archaeological remains into the sea.

NAVARRETE

The trip continues now towards Monte Cristi. After you've crossed the 1,300-m (4,265-ft) Cordillera Septentrional on the Carretera 5, you'll reach a roundabout 52km (32 miles) further on in

La Isabela cemetery

the town of **Navarrete** (which is marked on some maps as 'José E Bisonó'). The road to the left leads to Santiago, and the right one – the well-surfaced Carretera 1, also known as Carretera Duarte – to Monte Cristi.

From now on the route runs parallel to the Río Yaque del Norte across a broad, fertile plain; the main crops here are rice and tobacco. The barns used for drying the leaves can be seen throughout this region. On the right, the peaks of the Cordillera Septentrional are still visible; inland, the foothills of the Cordillera Central gradually come into view.

PUNTA RUCIA

In the small town of **Villa Elisa**, a not particularly well-surfaced road leads off to the right to **Punta Rucia** (around 25km/15 miles), a fishing village at the tip of a promontory, with attractive coastal vegetation and a quiet beach. There are excursions from Punta Rucia to the ruins of La Isabela. Ecoturisa *(see pages 114 and 118)* also organises trips to the ★★**Laguna Estero Hondo**. Visitors to the mangrove swamps here are sometimes lucky enough to spot that rarest of Caribbean animals, the manatee.

From Villa Elisa the dry landscape becomes quite spectacular. Agaves and cacti, some as high as 3m (10ft), grow in the sandy soil. The last stretch of the trip takes you past the final sandy foothills of the Cordillera Septentrional – and also past several goats who make a habit of wandering into the road.

MONTE CRISTI

Monte Cristi (pop. 20,000), capital of the province of the same name, is the last Dominican town in the northwest before the Haitian border. It was founded in 1533 by Juan de Bolaños and 60 other families who arrived here from the Canary Islands. By 1600, like Puerto Plata, it was almost completely deserted, and only began to prosper again in the 18th century. The numerous ramshackle-looking Victorian buildings bear witness to better days; those were at the turn of

Star Attraction
● Laguna Estero Hondo

Below: the road to Monte Cristi
Bottom: wayside goats

Map on pages 54–5

👁 **Gómez museum**

Monte Cristi was home to the revered general and freedom fighter, Máximo Gómez. Although born in the southern town of Baní, he settled in Monte Cristi and it was from here that he and the great Cuban patriot José Martí set sail to lead Cuba's war of independence from Spain. His house on Avenida Mella has mementos of his life and military career (open daily 9am–noon, 3–7pm).

Mangroves, Parque Nacional Monte Cristi

the century, when timber and agricultural produce were shipped from Monte Cristi to Europe.

The paint is peeling off the courthouse (corner of Avenida Duarte and Calle Federico Jesus Garcia), and the legal authorities have moved out of this formerly imposing Victorian building to a new concrete structure on the edge of town. Opposite the old courthouse on the left is the small municipal park, the Plaza del Reloj, named after the symbol of the town, a clock that originally came from France in 1895.

MANGROVES AND BEACHES

Drive up the small rise from the Plaza del Reloj and from the camouflaged barracks there's a good view across the very flat landscape surrounding the town. The only distinctive feature is the camel-hump mountain known as El Morro.

If you drive along the treeless promenade towards El Morro, past several salt-pans and *comedores* (roadside restaurants) you will see a thick mangrove swamp full of small waterways and, across to the left, the small island of Cabrita. The impression of having reached the end of the world is intensified if you follow the stony road up to where it forks: the route off to the left ends in the sea, beyond a small beach framed by weird-looking sandstone rocks.

Monte Cristi has several unremarkable sandy beaches, including Playa Juan de Bolaños (on the promenade) and Playa Granja, and the coastal waters here provide some of the best diving on the island, with both wrecks and coral reefs to explore.

NATIONAL PARK

You can take a boat excursion to the ★ **Parque Nacional Monte Cristi** (530sq km/205sq miles), which also takes in the group of islands known as Cayos Siete Hermanos. The park contains several rare birds and reptiles, including alligators. The mangroves' roots are a breeding-ground for many types of fish, and their branches are also a favourite nesting-place for seabirds.

4: High Mountains and Fertile Valleys

Puerto Plata – Santiago de los Caballeros – Moca – Salcedo – La Vega – (Jarabacoa – Constanza) – Bonao – Santo Domingo (240km/149 miles)

Map on page 68

As well as visiting the island's second city, Santiago, this route gives access to some dramatic scenery. There are several waterfalls, the best being the Salto de Jimenoa near Jarabacoa, while Pico Duarte, crowning the mighty Cordillera Central, is the highest mountain in the Caribbean.

SANTIAGO

From Puerto Plata, follow the Carretera 5 southwards for about 52km (32 miles). At the roundabout just before Navarrete, turn left. The Carretera Duarte continues towards Santiago at some distance from the Río Yaque del Norte. Soon, a forest of traffic signs along the roadside makes it clear that you're approaching a major centre, and after a further 10km (6 miles), **Santiago de los Caballeros** (pop. 700,000), the second largest town on the island, comes into view. Its name is derived from the 30 Spanish nobles *(caballeros)* who founded the town, along with Columbus's brother Bartolomé, in 1495. In fact, the town they founded, while they were

Below: Compañía Anónima Tabacalera logo, Santiago
Bottom: a street trader

Map below

searching the interior for gold, was a few miles northeast of its present-day location. After the severe earthquake of 1562 destroyed Santiago Viejo completely, the town was rebuilt on the eastern bank of the Río Yaque.

Santiago owes its prosperity first and foremost to rum and tobacco production; many Dominicans claim that the money spent in the capital,

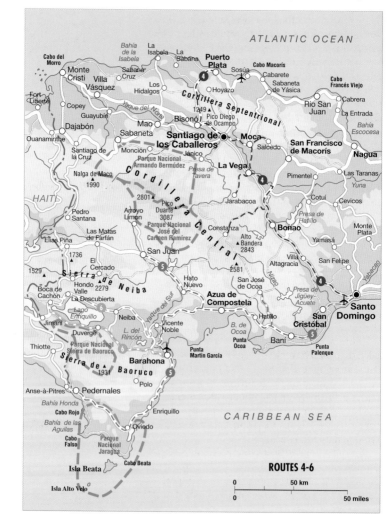

ROUTES 4-6

0   50 km

0   50 miles

Santo Domingo, is the money that's earned here, in the metropolis of the Cibao Valley.

SANTIAGO CATHEDRAL

The tour of Santiago begins at the fortress of San Luís, located on a small rise beside the river. In the early part of this century it was used as a prison; today it is a military barracks. There's a fine view of the valley, the bridge leading to San José de las Matas, and the more modern western part of the town from the river promenade, which is appropriately named the Avenida Mirador del Yaque.

Turn right about 700m further on, down the Calle 30 de Marzo, to reach the Parque Duarte. The south side of the square is dominated by the ★ **Catedral de Santiago Apóstol** (1868–95), a mixture of neo-Gothic and neoclassical styles. The three-aisled church contains a mahogany altar with gold-leaf decoration. Several notable national and regional figures, including the dictator Ulises Heureaux, lie buried in this church.

If you are interested in the present-day tobacco industry, the **Habanera Tabacalera**, just off Calle del Sol and five minutes from the former Museo del Tabaco, is a working tobacco factory, reputed to be the oldest *tabacalera* in the Dominican Republic. Here you can watch the entire process of manufacturing cigars from leaf to packaged luxury item (weekdays only). The factory is on the junction of San Luís and 16 de Agosto.

There is another cigar factory located on the edge of town on Avenida 27 de Febrero. The **León Jiménez Cigar Factory**, which celebrated its centenary in 2003, still produces hand made cigars using traditional methods. The guided tour around the modern complex is fascinating, even for non-smokers, and then you can browse in the factory shop afterwards.

Nearby is the **Centro Cultural Eduardo León Jiménez** (open 9am–6pm, closed Mon), a good display space for art exhibitions. The important centre is the leading exponent of Dominican art on the north coast.

Star Attraction
● Catedral de Santiago Apóstol

👁 **Mask museum**
Walk from the Parque Duarte north up the Calle Benito Monción and left into the Calle Restauración: you'll see a wooden building containing the **Museo Folklórico de Tomás Morel** (no fixed opening times). Inside there are all kinds of fantastic carnival masks and costumes. The carnival in Santiago is particularly famous, and on Sundays in February these masks can be seen in action.

At work in the cigar factory

Map
on page
68

PALACIO CONSISTORIAL

The **Centro de Recreo** is on the western side of the Parque Central. Built in neo-Mudéjar style in 1894, the building is occupied today by a private club; inside, the halls with their carved wooden ceilings bear mute witness to past glory.

The adjacent ★ **Palacio Consistorial** dates from the same period and is considered one of the finest 19th century structures on the island. Inside it, the **Casa de Cultura de Santiago** (open Mon–Sat 8am–6pm) has art exhibitions and cultural displays.

MERCADO MODELO

The Calle del Sol, Santiago's busy main shopping street, branches off from the northern side of the Parque Duarte. At the intersection with the Calle España is the white-and-green **Mercado Modelo**, which was built in the 1940s. All kinds of crafts can be bought in this two-storey building, including jewellery, ceramics, wooden figurines and wickerwork. As with all markets, try haggling.

Below: Bermúdez rum factory
Bottom: Palacio Consistorial

EL MONUMENTO

From here it's less than a mile eastwards up the Calle del Sol to the symbol of the town: the ★★ **Monumento a los Héroes de la Restauración de la República** (or 'El Monumento' for

short). This vast, white marble monument was built by Trujillo in the 1940s to commemorate the heroes who restored the Republic. It is 67m (220ft) high, and contains a museum as well as several works by Spanish painter, the late Vela Zanetti. The gigantic column contains a lift which takes visitors up to the observation platform, with its fantastic ★ **panoramic view**. Opposite, the **Teatro Nacional** is modelled on the national theatre in the capital, but is somewhat smaller.

You can wind up your tour of Santiago with a visit to the ★ **Bermúdez rum factory** (open Mon–Fri 9am–noon, 2–4pm) northwest of the town, on the corner of Avenida J Armando Bermúdez and Calle Blanca Mascaro. There are guided tours – and rum tastings.

MOCA

Located around 21km (13 miles) southeast of Santiago, **Moca** (pop. 50,000), the capital of the province of Espaillat, lies on a mountain slope at the centre of coffee and coconut plantations. The town was founded in the 18th century, and its neoclassical church of Nuestra Señora del Rosario next to the small Parque Central has interesting Gothic-style windows. If you follow the rather steep one-way street away from the centre towards the intersection for Salcedo and San Francisco de Macorís, to your left you'll see a small **locomotive** on a section of track in the Plaza Viaducto. It's a memorial to the Santiago–La Vega–Sánchez railroad that brought Moca prosperity at the beginning of the century.

Even though Moca has had little to do with the island's history, its inhabitants are still extremely proud of the fact that it was men from Moca who carried out the assassination of the dictator, Ulises Heureaux, in 1899.

SALCEDO

A well-surfaced road (Carretera 132) leads eastwards from Moca across 12km (7 miles) of delightful landscape filled with banana plants,

Star Attraction
● **El Monumento**

Party time
The area around the Monumento is the centre for outdoor partying and general festivities at weekends and on holidays. Despite complaints from residents and threats from the authorities, there are many informal rum shops, a lot of traffic and high-volume music. It's great fun – unless you are hoping to sleep anywhere in the vicinity.

El Monumento

Map on page 68

'The Butterflies'

The story of the three Mirabal sisters and their murder at Trujillo's hands is told in the novel *In the Time of the Butterflies* by the Dominican novelist Julia Alvarez. This poignant and atmospheric novel recreates the atmosphere of fear under Trujillo and the bravery of Patria, Minerva and Maria Teresa.

palm-trees and coconut palms. Like the rest of the Cibao Valley, this area is densely populated. Villages of colourfully-painted wooden houses line the road.

A detour off the beaten tourist track to **Salcedo** is highly worthwhile, not only for those interested in architecture but also because of its political history. At the entrance to the village is a square with a small modern metal sculpture. Portraits on the wall enclosing the square commemorate the *Tres Hermanas Mirabal*. They were placed here in 1990 for the 30th anniversary of the deaths of the three Mirabal sisters, who were shot by Trujillo's thugs on 25 November 1960, six months before his dictatorship came to an end.

Trujillo had already had thousands of Haitians and political opponents tortured and murdered, but it was his decision to have the daughters of a wealthy and highly-respected Dominican family killed that gave rise to a wave of indignation in the US. The memory of the Mirabal sisters is cherished in the Dominican Republic, particularly that of Minerva who stood up bravely to the dictator: stamps bear her likeness, and several streets are named after her.

About 5km (3 miles) beyond Salcedo on the road to Tenares and set back slightly on the right-hand side is the ★**Museo de las Hermanas Mirabal** (open 9.30am–5pm), containing many

Tres Hermanas Mirabal

photographs and personal belongings of the three sisters, Patria, Minerva and Maria Teresa, who died aged 36, 33 and 25; items include jewellery, clothing, a bloodstained handkerchief and the cap of their chauffeur who also died in the attack.

Below: devilish carnival mask
Bottom: Salcedo church

LA VEGA

Back in Moca, you can either make for the Carretera Duarte to reach La Vega, or take the Carretera 21 and possibly include excursions to the ruins of La Vega Vieja and to Santo Cerro *(see below)*.

The town of **La Vega** (pop. 55,000), also known as La Concepción de La Vega, lies only a few miles south of the place where Columbus had a fortress built in 1495 during his search for gold. On 2 December 1562, the town of La Concepción that had sprung up around it was destroyed in a severe earthquake, and was only re-founded in the 17th century, this time to the west of the Río Camú.

La Vega had its heyday when the railroad arrived here at the beginning of the 20th century. Its finest 19th century buildings, the Palacio de Justicia, the Teatro La Progresista and the Bombería (fire station), all date from that period.

In 1992, the rather pompous Nueva Catedral (corner of Calle Independencia and Calle Restauración) was completed. The architect of this enormous concrete church was evidently inspired by the stepped towers of the high Middle Ages – their function was to transport workers and materials high above cities. The Biblical number 12 plays a role here, too: the building has 12 portals and 12 windows.

A good time to visit La Vega is for either of the two annual carnivals (around 27 February and 16 August – *see page 106*). The celebrations are longer, more colourful and 'devilish' than elsewhere.

SANTO CERRO

An excursion can be made at this point from La Vega to the holy mountain of **Santo Cerro**, a centre of pilgrimage. Take the Carretera Duarte 8km

Map on page 68

Map on page 68

Divine intervention

An alternative version of the Santo Cerro legend recounts that in 1494 an expedition led by Columbus was confronted with a much larger and understandably aggressive force of Taínos. The Spanish looked to be losing the fight until Columbus planted his cross on the hilltop and the Virgin was seen to sit upon it. This miraculous apparition terrified the Taínos and encouraged the conquistadors, leading to their victory against the odds.

(5 miles) north and turn right at the small red signpost. A narrow asphalt track leads to a village with a church of early-colonial design but dating from 1886. Directly in front of it is a cross, and a tree next to it bears a plaque announcing that it came from the same tree that Christopher Columbus used to make the first ever crucifix here.

And thereby hangs a tale: in 1495 the Taínos rose up against their Spanish overlords on the Santo Cerro under the leadership of Guarionex. Just as they were about to set fire to the cross placed here by Columbus – so the story goes – the Virgen de las Mercedes appeared, protected the Christian symbol and forced the Indians to subjugate themselves. A section of the original cross is apparently preserved inside the church.

It's certainly worth going round the back to enjoy the extraordinary ★ **view** across the valley, which Columbus named *La Vega Real* ('The Royal Meadows').

Big country near La Vega

LA VEGA VIEJA

A steep section of road lined with statues of saints leads back down the other side of Santo Cerro and across to the Carretera 21 (the La Vega–Moca road). Turn left in the direction of Pueblo Viejo. Look out for a turning on the left by a battered signpost to the ruins of **La Vega Vieja**, a settlement originally founded in 1494 by Columbus, but destroyed by an earthquake in 1562.

Fortaleza Nuestra Señora de la Concepción (open most days, and weekends, 9am–2pm) is the fortress built by Columbus after his victory over the Taínos in 1495. One tower, with arrow slits, is quite well preserved, but most of the ruins are overgrown. A museum nearby contains several everyday items, both Taíno and Spanish, that were unearthed on the site. The **Ruinas Convento San Francisco** are the remains of the Franciscan monastery, built in 1502. The foundation walls show the outlines of different sections of the first monastery built on American soil; the chapel, the well and the cloister. There is also a cemetery nearby and the area is a national historical park.

DETOUR TO JARABACOA

To see a totally different kind of landscape, it's worth making a ★ **detour to Jarabacoa** (pop. 30,000; 526m/1,725ft). The distance there and back to La Vega is 54km (33 miles), and the route leads along the foot of the Cordillera Central. Around 3km (2 miles) north of La Vega there's a turn-off from the Autopista Duarte. The road's condition is good, and soon it starts to get very steep as it makes its way up the **Alpes Dominicanos**, a popular holiday destination for the island's inhabitants. The mountain town is a centre for adventure tourism, which attracts visitors looking for a hiking, or biking challenge. Others come to paddle the rivers as part of an organised kayaking, canyoning or rafting trip.

Nestling among pine forests and the valleys of the Río Yaque del Norte and Río Jimenoa, Jarabacoa enjoys springtime temperatures almost the whole year round.

There are several natural sights to see here. One is the ★★ **Salto de Jimenoa** waterfall. The water cascades 20m (65ft) and you can take a refreshing shower underneath. Access to the falls is via a series of flimsy-looking bridges suspended high above the water. The best way to get there is on a trip organised by one of the local hotels (Pinar Dorado, tel: 809 574 2820 or Rancho Baiguate, tel: 809 574 4940).

Star Attraction
● **Salto de Jimenoa**

Below: Salto de Jimenoa
Bottom: main highway, Jarabacoa

Map on page 68

Arduous climb

Climbing the Pico Duarte is no stroll. It is essential that you hire reliable guides (such as those provided by the Rancho Baiguate) and that you are prepared for an arduous three-day trek. There are no facilities, and climbers must take food, water and warm clothing, as temperatures can fall below freezing at night. The best months are between November and March when there is less chance of heavy rain.

Pico Duarte

POOLS AND PEAKS

Another good place to visit is the ★ **Balneario La Confluencia**, 2km (1mile) from Jarabacoa, a natural swimming pool created by the confluence of the Río Yaque del Norte and the Río Jimenoa. The shallow water here is particularly popular with the Dominicans during holiday season, when several stalls are set up to serve open-air snacks.

Or you could go on an excursion to **Salto de Baiguate**, a waterfall with a natural swimming pool. It can be reached only along a particularly rough track, so it's advisable to use either a jeep or a horse. Book your trip through the Hotel Rancho Baiguate.

It takes between two and four days to scale the nearby ★★ **Pico Duarte** (3,087m/10,128ft), the highest peak in the Caribbean. The Pico Duarte lies at the southern edge of the Parque Nacional Armando Bermúdez which, together with the Parque Nacional José Carmen Ramírez next door, covers a total surface area of 1,530sq km (590sq miles) of rain forest. Visitors are not permitted to enter the national parks without an official guide and a permit, so if you wish to climb the peak plan ahead.

DETOUR TO CONSTANZA

The direct route between Jarabacoa and Constanza is a bumpy track. You could just make the rough ride, which takes about 2½ hours, with a normal car. However, it is more comfortable to drive back to the Autopista Duarte and carry on in the direction of Santo Domingo (104km/64 miles round trip).

About 33km (20 miles) beyond La Vega, just as you're entering the village of El Abánico, the Carretera 12 branches off next to the Parador Los Quatro Vientos hotel. This road snakes its way steeply up the mountain to an altitude of 1,220m (4,000ft). In the valley below you can see the Rincón Reservoir sparkling in the sunlight, and eventually the fertile high plateau comes into view: a Garden of Eden with coffee plantations, exotic flowers and fields planted with many kinds of vegetables. The mild climate here means that even apples, strawberries and peaches can be successfully cultivated.

Constanza itself (1,100m/3,609ft above sea-level) doesn't have a lot to offer although the location is beautiful, with rivers, waterfalls and forests on the mountains surrounding the circular valley, formed by a meteor. There are a few restaurants and some small hotels, but the place is very quiet. In December and January it's quite common for night time temperatures to sink below freezing. The nearby valleys and mountains are ideal for hiking trips, and the waterfalls at **Aguas Blancas**, around 10km (6 miles) to the south are also worth a visit.

BONAO

After this detour, the way back to Santo Domingo passes via **Bonao** (pop. 50,000), capital of the province of Monseñor Nouel. The town lies just off the main road, but there's no need to leave it to find out what Bonao is famous for: all kinds of ceramic and agricultural products can be bought from stalls along the roadside.

The nearby Falconbridge nickel mine was the second largest in the world until 1988. From Bonao it's another 85km (53 miles) back to Santo Domingo (see page 24).

Star Attraction
● Pico Duarte

Below: Constanza girl
Bottom: terraced cultivation near Constanza

5: The Southwest

Santo Domingo – San Cristóbal – Baní – Azua de Compostela – Barahona – Parque Nacional Jaragua – Pedernales (289km/180 miles)

The Autopista Sánchez leads into the least touristy southwest of the country. It's drier than the north, the vegetation isn't as green and is much sparser. Allow a week for the trip to Pedernales and back, because there is a lot to see: relics from the pre-Columbian era, the heritage of colonialism, sites of historic battles fought in the 19th century, most of them against the Haitians, the Jaragua National Park and, last but not least, mile upon mile of untouched, beautiful beaches, especially the section between Barahona and Pedernales.

Below: Nuestra Señora de Consolación
Bottom: Paraíso beach near Barahona

SAN CRISTOBAL

Leave Santo Domingo and head west on the Malecón, which will take you straight to the four-lane Carretera Sánchez toll road. Pass the entrance to the Bajos de Haina container terminal, cross the Río Haina, and travel another 25km (15 miles) or so to the town of **San Cristóbal** (pop. 150,000) on the Río Nigua, capital of the province of the same name. It's a busy market town and trading centre, and is named after some fortifications built by Bartolomé Colón at the beginning of the 16th

century to protect the gold discovered at the mouths of the Haina and Nigua rivers.

The town as we know it today was founded at the beginning of the 19th century. On 6 November 1844, San Cristóbal was the scene of an important moment in history: it was here that the Dominican revolutionary government ratified the country's first constitution.

DICTATOR'S BIRTHPLACE

The town is more notorious than famous for being the birthplace of Rafael Leonidas Trujillo y Molina (1891–1961) who, as the dictator 'General Trujillo', ruled the Dominican Republic from 1930 to 1961. He heaped honours and honorary titles on to the town. One of Trujillo's legacies is the neo-classical church of **Parroquia de Nuestra Señora de Consolación**, which was built in 1946. Like the Town Hall (where the constitution was signed in 1844) it lies close to the Parque Central.

Trujillo used this church for much self-glorification; the dictator's ornate chair still stands in front of the mahogany altar. Trujillo's corpse lay in state in the basement of this building for a short while following his assassination in 1961, but after local protests it was transferred to France. The burial vault of the Trujillo family, entered via a wrought-iron door, contains several other tombs and statues of saints. A memorial outside the church marks the presumed location of the house where the Generalísimo was born.

TRUJILLO'S HOUSES

There are several examples of the dictator's architectural legacy outside the town centre, too. About 5km (3 miles) to the north in the direction of La Toma is his former country seat, **Casa de la Caoba**. This ruined villa, the first floor of which was lined with mahogany *(caoba)*, is located on a hill with a fine view of the surrounding landscape. A few miles to the north of the Casa Caoba, Trujillo had a private swimming pool and bathing complex built; today anyone can swim in the

Home town boy
With the same modesty that led him to rename Santo Domingo 'Ciudad Trujillo', the dictator decided that his home town was in need of a new name and decided on Ciudad Benemérita or 'Meritorious City'. Some older residents might have been wise not to share their memories of the younger Trujillo, who developed an unsavoury reputation as a cattle thief and petty criminal before rising up the ranks of the US-trained Guardia Nacional.

Parque Central, San Cristóbal

Map on page 68

Map on page 68

The Guardians
The ruins of Casa de la Caoba and the Palacio del Cerro both have local guardians, who will let visitors in to have a look around. However, be warned, they will expect a tip.

Balneario La Toma (open Mon–Fri 9am–6pm, Sat–Sun 7am–7.30pm).

Located on a rise to the west of the town is the **Palacio del Cerro**. This fortress-like palace, built in the 1950s, was never actually occupied by Trujillo. The lift stuck regularly, and the dark frescoes by the Spanish painter the late Vela Zanetti were not to the dictator's taste.

Fifteen kilometres (9 miles) north of San Cristóbal are the caves of **El Pomier**, where thousands of Taíno inscriptions and pictograms can be seen. The drawings show scenes from daily life as well as religious themes. Long under threat from quarrying, the caves are now protected; ramps, walkways and lighting have been installed.

NIGUA AND NAJAYO

San Cristóbal is a good starting-point for two excursions (though unfortunately the roads for both are very badly surfaced). The first is to the small town of **Nigua**, 11km (7 miles) south of San Cristóbal. The beach here is like any other, but the highlights are the two ★ **sugar mills** dating from the colonial era. One of them, Boca de Nigua, is still partially intact. The mill, in which the sugar cane was crushed by a mill-wheel driven by oxen, can be clearly recognised, as can the boiling house with its hearths. The other factory, Diego Caballero, is a few minutes' walk further west, and is older. Only a few foundation walls remain, but the setting is picturesque.

The second excursion from San Cristóbal is 14km (9 miles) to the south: the beach at **Najayo**, which is popular with locals, and also the Playa Palenque 6km (4 miles) further west. At weekends there's a great atmosphere in the bars at the beach.

BANI

The route now continues across the Río Nizao in the province of Peravia and via its capital ★ **Baní** (pop. 40,000). The name is derived from an old Indian word meaning 'the town rich in water'. Thanks to this, agriculture plays an all-important role here. Sugar cane has been

Sugar cane factory

cultivated in the Baní region since the colonial era, but the first settlement was only established here in the 18th century, founded by immigrants from the Canary Islands who lived mainly off livestock production. Today, Baní is a very clean and well-kept town with an attractive centre.

Máximo Gómez, the Cuban freedom-fighter, was born in Baní on 18 November 1836 and died on Castro Island in 1905. A memorial to Gómez is in the small park laid out in the Calle Máximo Gómez, with a statue in the middle. At the back of the park is a small house, **La Casa de Máximo Gómez**, which has a general history of the period, photos and historical documents.

LAS SALINAS

One interesting excursion from Baní is a trip north (20km/12 miles) along the Río Baní via El Recodo to Limonal, where there's a great view across the Valdesia Reservoir. Those keen on crashing waves and flying spray should go to the **Playa Baní** 7km (4 miles) south of the town.

There are more peaceful beaches with extensive dunes about 20km (12 miles) to the west in Las Calderas, and also on the small ★★ **Las Salinas Peninsula**, named after the local salt-pans; this area, protected as a national monument, has grown very popular with windsurfers.

Star Attraction
● **Las Salinas Peninsula**

Below and bottom:
salt miners and their huts
in Las Salinas

Surprising stalls

The hot, dry road from Baní to Azua is an unlikely site for a roadside market, but at a place called Boquerón, clustered around a military checkpoint, you are likely to find a collection of stalls selling fruit and vegetables as well as hand-made pestles and mortars and brooms.

SAN JOSE AND HATILLO

From Baní the Carretera 2 leads through increasingly barren-looking landscape. After 12km (7 miles) a road branches off northwards; those not in a hurry at this point can take a detour along a well-surfaced road (Carretera 41) to ★ **San José de Ocoa** (pop. 25,000), around 76km/47 miles there and back. Set in attractive, lush green landscape, San José was founded in the 17th century by several runaway slaves *(cimarrones)*. The pleasant, mild climate promotes the growth of fruit and vegetables around the town, particularly figs and potatoes.

After this detour into the 'cooler' regions, continue along the Carretera Sánchez to **Hatillo**. This little village lies at the foot of the mountain known as El Número, which in 1849 was the scene of the last battle between the Dominicans and the Haitians. General Duvergé's army inflicted such a heavy defeat on the Haitian troops here that they never dared set foot on Dominican soil again. From Hatillo a rough track leads south to the Bay of Ocoa, with its shallow waters and attractive coral. The fishing village of **Palmar de Ocoa** attracts deep sea fishermen.

Courthouse and ice-cream parlour, Azua

AZUA

The provincial capital of **Azua de Compostela** (pop. 85,000) lies at the centre of a prosperous and well-irrigated agricultural area. Melons are a particularly popular crop in this region of low precipitation. The town began as a settlement that was founded by Diego Velázquez in 1504, nearer the sea and 15km (9 miles) to the south. The harbour soon began competing with Santo Domingo, and Azua de Compostela was given its official charter in 1508. From 1505 to 1511 Hernán Cortés, who later conquered Mexico, was the town clerk here.

Azua was actually destroyed by the French shortly afterwards in 1538, but then rebuilt. Then, in 1791, it was a tidal wave following an earthquake that obliterated the town. Canarian settlers later rebuilt Azua on its present site. It was attacked by Haiti on several occasions during the Haitian-Dominican wars, and set ablaze in 1849 by the dictator Faustín Soulouque's retreating troops after their defeat at El Número.

A monument stands in Azua's **Parque Central** in memory of the battle that took place on 19 March 1844, when the town successfully defended itself against attack by Haitian troops.

INDIAN HERO

Near the barracks there's another memorial to a different battle: it's in honour of the Indian chief Guarocuya, baptised Enriquillo, who for 14 years put up successful resistance to the Spanish colonists in this area and forced a peace agreement with the colonial forces in 1533. Many Azuanos are proud to be descended from the Taínos who settled this part of the island after the peace treaty.

Below: balcony scene, Azua
Bottom: merengue evening in Peralta

The attractive beach at Azua, known as Monte Río (7km/4 miles southeast), is usually very crowded; avoid it if you are looking for solitude and tranquillity.

In the old harbour of ★ **Puerto Viejo**, 15km (9 miles) to the south, several remnants from the colonial period can be seen. To the north of Azua, the small mountain town of ★ **Peralta** on the banks of the Río Jura, surrounded by coffee plantations, is very pretty.

Map on page 68

Festival town
San Juan de la Maguana is famous for its religious festivals, including a spectacular Altagracia procession on 21 January and Holy Week, when the town is filled with crowds celebrating not only Christian Easter but also Taíno spirits. The *fiesta patronal* of San Juan takes place from 15 to 24 June and involves much live music and rum drinking.

Larimar *outlet, Barahona*

A worthwhile excursion from Azua is to the region around the town of **San Juan de la Maguana**. This is a thriving agricultural area, with many tobacco, rice and banana plantations. To the north of the attractive little town is a remnant of Indian culture, the Corral de los Indios. This reconstruction of a holy shrine consists of a gravestone with a carved face, surrounded by a stone circle.

BARAHONA

On the trip from Azua to Barahona there are cacti as far as the eye can see, many of them growing gorgeous flowers. On the western shore of the Bahía de Neiba, the steppe-like landscape gradually changes into the fertile delta region of the Río Yaque del Sur, and soon **Barahona** (pop. 70,000) comes into view. This provincial capital lives mainly off its harbour, which is dominated by a defunct sugar-mill. Products shipped here include salt, wood, wax, minerals such as the semi-precious *larimar*, which is mined nearby, and agricultural produce. In 1997 a technical university was opened here.

SAFE HARBOUR

In the 17th century the Bay of Neiba, on which the town lies, was a favourite haunt of pirates; it was protected from the open sea by reefs and also virtually inaccessible by land. The notorious Cofresí is thought to have hidden here at one point. The town was founded by General Toussaint l'Ouverture who travelled eastwards from Haiti in 1802. The Haitian ruler developed a thriving port, mainly for the export of local hard woods, such as mahogany.

It has quite a few wooden houses, and its church seems in imminent danger of collapsing; otherwise there isn't much to see. The main meeting place for the locals is the **Parque Central**, where there are several restaurants and a disco. The long beach promenade is not very attractive, and the small municipal beach is polluted.

DESERTED BEACHES

In contrast, beyond Barahona there is a beautiful section of coast road, which has recently been greatly improved. The broad, smooth asphalt road runs south; to the right are the foothills of the Baoruco Mountains, and to the left a series of deserted beaches and bays. About 10km (6 miles) further on there's a left turn to the **Playa El Quemaito**, and after another 20km (12 miles) is the **Playa San Rafael**.

A small stream meets the sea at the magnificent sandy beach here, so there's the choice between a freshwater or a seawater swim. Freshly-caught fish is served in the wooden huts. A word of warning: in bad weather, falling rocks can be a hazard in this bay.

JARAGUA NATIONAL PARK

Continue now to **Baoruco**, with its large hotel, and then on to ★★**Paraíso**. Located on a bay at the mouth of the Río Nizalta, the latter really is delightful. The beach promenade is lined by small terraced houses made of stone.

Beyond Enriquillo the land starts getting flatter. Pasture appears, and the towns and villages are farther apart. Beside the road on the left, just before the rather gloomy-looking village of Oviedo comes into view, is the administration

Star Attraction
● Paraíso

Below: Barahona fire station
Bottom: palm trees at Paraíso

Map on page 68

Huts in the Baoruco rainforest

building for the ★★ **Parque Nacional Jaragua** (1,350sq km/521sq miles), the largest national park in the country. It covers the entire southern part of the Baoruco Peninsula, including the islands of Isla Beata and Alto Velo.

This palm- and cactus-filled nature reserve contains several caves and the remains of Jaragua Indian settlements, after which the park is named. The flora and fauna are incredibly varied. More than half of all the bird species native to the island can be found here, including the almost extinct Hispaniola buzzard. There are several species of rare turtle, too. The park may be entered only with a guide and a permit, obtainable from the central park administration in Santo Domingo *(see page 114)* or the local park office.

PEDERNALES

From Oviedo, the Carretera 44 leads northwest in the direction of the Haitian border. After a 48-km (30-mile) drive with hardly anything coming in the opposite direction, you'll see the turning to the small harbour and fishing village of **Cabo Rojo**. If you have plenty of time on your hands, ask your way to the ★ **Playa Aguila**; its 2km-long beaches are definitely worth the extra trip.

The town of **Pedernales**, capital of Pedernales province and not far from the border, has little of cultural interest to offer. It's famous for its bauxite, the raw material used to make aluminium. The municipal beach is unattractive, with no palm trees and therefore no shade. However the coast near the town is very popular with divers and snorkellers.

North of Pedernales runs an extremely rough mountain road (4-wheel drive only) that skirts the border with Haiti. If passable (check with locals), it eventually emerges at the village of **El Naranjo** and then leads to Jimaní *(see page 89)*. Crossing over the Sierra de Baoruco, this track leads adventurous visitors through some of the country's wildest scenery, where pine forests and subtropical rainforests are home to countless species of flora. The area is earmarked for development, but at present is far from the beaten tourism track.

6: Around Lake Enriquillo

**Barahona – Neiba – Las Cabritos – Jimaní –
Duvergé – Barahona (208km/129 miles)**

One of the most attractive regions of the Dominican Republic is the area around Lake Enriquillo. The salt lake, surrounded by the mountains of the Sierra de Neiba and the Sierra de Baoruco, lies at the bottom of a natural basin almost 40m (130ft) below sea-level (the lowest point in the Caribbean). The region is hot and dry, but very fertile, too, thanks to numerous springs and small rivers. The temperatures are around 9°F (5°C) higher than the areas of the country close to the sea. The ★★ **Sierra de Baoruco National Park** has all kinds of different vegetation levels up to an altitude of 2,300m (7,500ft) and almost 50 species of bird, as well as rare butterflies. The driest zones contain not only cacti but also pine and even deciduous forests.

Star Attraction
● **Parque Nacional Jaragua**
● **Sierra de Baoruco**

Orchid paradise
The Sierra de Baoruca National Park, 800sq km (300sq miles) in area, is thought to have been formed from crystallised limestone some 500 million years ago. With its climate ranging from desert to mountain rainforest, it is home to no fewer than 166 species of orchid – more than half of those found in the Dominican Republic. Of these, 32 are found only in this wilderness.

LAKE ENRIQUILLO

The starting-point for this tour is **Barahona**. Reliable guides can be found in the hotels; they take visitors to the main places of interest and point out interesting details in return for a small fee.

Leave Barahona *(see page 84)* on the Carretera 44 in a northwesterly direction then, after 12km

Lake Enriquillo

Map on page 68

Friendly reptiles

The iguanas on the Isla Cabritos are tame and will readily approach human visitors, although feeding them is strictly discouraged. The crocodiles are much more shy and tend to congregate at the northwestern tip of the lake, where fresh water enters from a river near La Descubierta.

Caves of Las Caritas

(7 miles), take the Carretera 48 to the left, across the Río Yaque del Sur. This region is full of sugar cane. Pass the small village of Tamayo and then cross the foothills of the Sierra de Neiba to reach **Neiba**, a friendly market town which is known for its grapes, sold on the main square in season.

Soon after the village of Villa Jaragua, the enormous ★★**Lake Enriquillo** comes into view for the first time. Its shallow salt water – three times saltier than the sea because of steady evaporation – lies immobile in the sunshine. The lake is 42km (26 miles) long and 12km (7 miles) wide, and its bed is covered with a thick layer of ancient shells and fossilised coral.

ENRIQUILLO'S HIDEAWAY

Near Postrer Río, on the right above the road, there are some remnants of Taíno culture in the **Caves of Las Caritas**. Those who feel strong enough to make the 50-m (164-ft) ascent will be rewarded by several very interesting scratch-marks on the cave walls resembling faces; some are only rough outlines, others are more detailed. Enriquillo, the Indian leader, and his men are thought to have sought refuge here from the Spanish. Strategically, the caves are well located: from up here you can see across the entire island.

NATIONAL PARK

A few hundred metres away is the administration office of the ★★**Parque Nacional Isla Cabritos**. The 'Isle of Goats', 12km (7 miles) long and 2km (1 mile) wide, is the largest of the three islands in the lake. Its remoteness has turned it into a natural paradise, supporting an abundance of wildlife. Flamingoes, giant iguanas and even American crocodiles live here. From the park office it's possible to be taken by boat with a guide. The trip from the mainland to the island takes 45 minutes. On the island there is an information centre, a small museum and three trails from where you can see the crocodiles.

LA DESCUBIERTA AND JIMANI

The next stop on this route is **La Descubierta**, which is a green oasis backed by the rugged Sierra de Neiba. The reason it exists is the nearby swimming area *(balneario)* of Las Barías, with its lake fed by underground springs. This is a good place to sit and watch children swimming, women washing clothes and elderly people chatting away in the shade of the palm trees. Simple food is also served from a small palm-roofed kitchen.

The border town of **Jimaní** at the western end of the lake appears reasonably prosperous, but at the same time extremely quiet. The border post, 7km (4 miles) away, is a hive of inactivity: the soldiers look bored, and apart from the odd *tap-tap* (multi-coloured Haitian bus) bringing day-workers to the border and back from Haiti, there's nothing much going on *(see page 90)*.

LAGUNA DEL RINCON

The Carretera 46 follows the southern shore of the lake. Just before **Duvergé** on the left is the small *balneario* of La Zurza; 5km (3 miles) beyond the village there's a turning to Neiba. At the junction is the imposing-looking memorial to the Taíno chieftain Enriquillo, 'the first fighter for independence in the New World', who struggled against the Spanish colonists for 14 years *(see*

Star Attractions
● Lake Enriquillo
● Isla Cabritos

Below: the road to Neiba
Bottom: La Descubierta

Map on page 68

'Magnetic pole'
To experience an odd optical illusion, turn right into the mountains at the village of Cabral, towards a settlement called Polo. Before you reach the village there is a signposted stretch of road, called the Polo Magnético. The road appears to slope uphill, but a car left in neutral will run forward, apparently defying gravity.

Survivor in a harsh environment

page 19). Continue now via Mella in the direction of a little village called Cabral.

Before you get there, the ★ **Laguna del Rincón** comes into view on the left-hand side. A 5-m (16-ft) deep freshwater lake extending across an area of 30sq km (12sq miles), it is home to innumerable flamingoes and cormorants, and also turtles (*jicotea*). The Laguna del Rincón is the second largest lake in the country, and is fed by small streams and rainwater. The starting-point of this route, Barahona, is now only a few miles away.

ACROSS THE BORDER

Adventurous visitors may want to cross the border into neighbouring Haiti. There are, of course, easier and more comfortable ways of reaching Haiti, with regular flights and air-conditioned buses leaving from Santo Domingo. But it is an unusual experience to walk across the frontier.

There are various crossing points: of the four main border towns – Dajabón, Jimaní, Pedernales and Elias Piña – only the first two officially allow foreigners to cross into Haiti and back. In Pedernales and Elias Piña, there are informal arrangements, as there are no immigration offices, and a $10 'tip' is usually sufficient to persuade military personnel to turn a blind eye. Similar payments have to be made to Haitian officials – and on returning. But this is a rather risky procedure, and travellers have been stranded on returning late and finding a different officer in charge.

CROSSING AT JIMANI

Jimaní is an authorised border crossing, and your passport will be duly stamped on payment of a departure tax of $10. The same fee will be expected at the Haitian border post, and a further $10 will be necessary to re-enter the Dominican Republic.

The actual border, known ominously as Mal Paso ('bad crossing'), is a bleak and scorchingly hot no man's land some two miles from Jimaní. *Públicos* and *motoconchos* shuttle to and fro, and it is easy to reach the crossing point. Strangely, there is a large market held here on most days, selling Haitian rum and counterfeit designer goods. This is a colourful and noisy affair, with a good deal of haggling going on.

Across the border, the landscape is as uninviting as on the Dominican side. The Haitian settlement of **Malpasse** is no more than a cluster of buildings, but you will be able to hire a motorbike taxi to take you to the nearby **Etang Saumâtre**, another large, brackish lake like Enriquillo, with extensive bird life and crocodiles. There are isolated villages and smallholdings in this arid area of Haiti, but little of cultural interest.

Below: cacti near Lake Enriquillo
Bottom: border crossing at Jimaní

CROSSING AT DAJABON

The best place to cross the border in terms of Haitian interest is further north at **Dajabón**, which can be easily reached from Monte Cristi. Here there is another colourful border market on Mondays and Fridays, and across the frontier lies the town of **Ouanaminthe**. From here it is 20 km (12 miles) by taxi to **Fort Liberté**, a small, run-down coastal town sitting on a wide bay. Nearby is Fort Dauphin, built in 1732 by the French, a crumbling stone complex of fortifications and a ruined chapel. It is a poignant reminder of the importance once accorded to the colony of Saint-Domingue.

Map below

Map below

King Sugar

Elsewhere in the country, the sugar industry has fallen on hard times since its heyday at the beginning of the 20th century, and the government is keen to sell off land for other purposes. But the area around La Romana and San Pedro de Macorís is still ruled by 'King Sugar', as revealed by vistas of sugar cane, squalid *bateyes* (canecutters' settlements) and rusting refineries.

7: From Sugar to Tourism

Santo Domingo – La Caleta – Boca Chica – San Pedro de Macorís – La Romana (102km/63 miles)

The southeast coast is relatively densely populated, with a lot of tourist development. In contrast to the southwest, remote and isolated beaches are rare, and there are quite a few high-standard hotels. The traditional source of income for this part of the Dominican Republic is the sugar industry, but tourism is now more profitable. The drive to La Romana can be done in a day.

AMERICAN HIGHWAY

Take the four-lane Autopista de las Américas eastwards from Santo Domingo. The name of the road actually derives from the 21 alphabetically-arranged, rather battered plaques along the side of the road bearing the names of the 21 countries of Latin America.

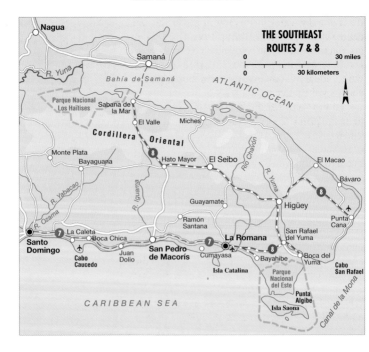

THE SOUTHEAST
ROUTES 7 & 8

LA CALETA

In **La Caleta**, 20km (12 miles) into the trip, a road branches off to Las Américas Airport, the largest in the country.

Off the harbour at La Caleta, the hulks of two wrecked ships were sunk in order to create an artificial reef. Boats now take divers out to this protected underwater area, known as the ★ **Parque Submarino**; its banks of coral are home to numerous colourful species of tropical fish.

Star Attraction
● **Parque Submarino**

On the beach at Boca Chica

BOCA CHICA

Travel along the Carretera Mella to the European-style tourist resort of **Boca Chica** – one of the least restful places on the island. The streets are full of hawkers, and the beach, though attractive, is so full at weekends that it's hard to find a space to yourself. It was Trujillo who first made this place famous when he had a hotel built beside the beach.

Known as 'the largest swimming pool in the Caribbean', the reef-protected bay – ideal for family fun and a variety of watersports – is never deeper than 1.5m (5ft). Today, Boca Chica, with all its hotels and restaurants, is probably the noisiest resort on the island, and perfect for those whose ideal holiday involves non-stop nightlife and very little sleep.

Continue past the quiet beach of Guayacanes to **Juan Dolio**. There aren't any sights to see in this modern resort, which has become a centre of package-holiday tourism in the past few years, but diving and windsurfing courses are available.

SAN PEDRO DE MACORIS

It's only another 15km (9 miles) now from Juan Dolio to ★ **San Pedro de Macorís** (pop. 90,000), the fourth-largest town in the country and named after the Macorís Indians who once populated this region. San Pedro lies at the mouth of the Río Iguamo, which is spanned here by a massive bridge. Keep right on the other side of the bridge and you'll arrive at the centre of this town, founded in 1822.

Map on page 92

Baseball

San Pedro de Macorís is the heartland of Dominican baseball and home to such legends as Sammy Sosa. You cannot avoid seeing children practising their skills on any empty piece of land, while the huge Tetelo Vargas stadium in the northern barrio of Restauración attracts big crowds to watch professional games during the winter season. Baseball has created huge fortunes for a lucky few and is seen by many Dominicans as the dream ticket out of poverty.

Fire station, San Pedro de Macorís

There is a *zona franca* (free-trade zone) here, and agriculture also plays an important role. Sugar cane isn't as important as it used to be; at the beginning of this century San Pedro was the heart of the Dominican sugar industry. Hundreds of miles of railway tracks connected the sugar factories across the country with its harbour. When the world sugar price increased sharply after World War I, San Pedro became incredibly prosperous.

REMAINS OF AFFLUENCE

There are few visible remnants of that time of glory in the town today, but those that do remain are still worth a visit. From the **Parque Duarte**, walk westwards along the Avenida Independencia in the direction of the river promenade and several architectural jewels of the good old days will come into view: the Victorian-style **fire station** on the Calle Duarte, which was built by the Hamburg-America line between 1903 and 1906; or the former **Parliament Building** on the corner of Duarte and Sánchez, today an ironmonger's.

On the river promenade at the end of the Avenida Independencia is the striking-looking church of **San Pedro Apóstol** (1908–13). The tower is decorated with Gothic-style gargoyles, and there's also a medieval-looking rose window. The three-aisled interior contains an elaborately carved mahogany altar.

San Pedro de Macorís's close links with its past are nowhere more evident than in the festival of St Peter, held every 29 June. The celebrations feature dances known as *gouloyas*, which date back to African rites and were brought over by labourers employed in the British Antilles *(see page 103)*. Known familiarly as *cocolos*, these workers were needed because the local population was unable to cope with the sheer amount of labour involved in the sugar harvest.

The Carretera 3 now leads eastwards, passing the baseball stadium of Tetelo Vargas, where the municipal market has established itself opposite. On the outskirts of town turn left, and continue into open countryside past pasture and sugar cane plantations.

WONDROUS CAVES

The **Reserva Antropológica de las Cuevas de las Maravillas** (open Tues–Sun 10am–6pm) is off the main San Pedro de Macorís to La Romana road, and well worth a visit. Knowledgeable guides conduct one-hour tours through the vast cave system, where you can see stalagmites and stalactites. The caves were used by the Taíno Indians and their drawings can be seen along the well-lit walkways. Maintenance work can force temporary closure of the site, where there is also a museum and café.

Below: La Romana bungalow
Bottom: a local work of art

LA ROMANA

Beyond the rivers Soco and Cumayasa (there's a small road leading to the attractive beach at Cumayasa just before the bridge) is the provincial capital of **La Romana** (pop. 100,000). The enormous Central de La Romana sugar mill, the largest employer in these parts, can be seen from far and wide. La Romana only began to develop in the mid-19th century, and it owes much of its prosperity to Cuban sugar producers and also to the North American Gulf & Western Company, which bought up vast tracts of land for sugar cane cultivation during the 1920s.

The small **park** with its obelisks in the Avenida Libertad is a haven of tranquillity in the busy town. The brightly-painted wooden houses in this

Map on page 92

Below: boat trip, Río Chavón
Bottom: Altos de Chavón

area belong to the more wealthy employees of the sugar trade. The areas round the town centre are poorer. The Parque Central has its usual town hall and parish church; above the church is the Mercado Municipal, an entire district full of shops and stalls where it's very easy to get lost.

ISLA CATALINA

It's just a 20-minute boat trip from La Romana's small harbour to the ★ **Isla Catalina**. The beaches have fine, white sand with some of the best bathing in waters protected by reefs. Diving is also excellent, but there is no need to get your feet wet if you don't want to: the diving grounds can also be admired through glass-bottomed boats.

ALTOS DE CHAVON

The exclusive tourist complex of Casa de Campo, on the eastern edge of La Romana, has three world-class golf courses, a millionaire clientele and prices to match. Linked to it is a fascinating cultural sight: the ★★ **Altos de Chavón**, a replica 16th-century Mediterranean village situated on a hill above the Río Chavón with a great panoramic view. There's the small church of San Estanislao, an **amphitheatre** with a seating capacity of 3,000 and an ★ **archaeological museum** (open daily 9am–5pm) with some fascinating exhibits documenting Taíno culture.

The amphitheatre was inaugurated with a concert by Frank Sinatra, and various luminaries such as Gloria Estefan and Julio Iglesias have appeared there, as well as top Dominican performers. There is a range of accommodation in Altos de Chavón, which also contains a School of Design, a branch of the Parsons School in New York. Scholarship holders from all over the world can study here in a uniquely beautiful environment. There are galleries, craft shops, and restaurants of all kinds. Altos de Chavón is open to everyone and definitely worth a visit. Note, however, that the prices of food and drink are somewhat higher here than elsewhere on the island.

8: The Southeast

La Romana – Bayahibe – Higüey – Sabana de la Mar (169km/105 miles)

The highlights of this route include the crystal-clear blue waters of the Parque Nacional del Este, with its fascinating island of Saona, the pilgrimage town of Higüey, and the sleepy little town of Sabana de la Mar, with its optional detour to the Samaná Peninsula or to the Los Haïtises National Park. The remote beaches near the comfortable resorts of Punta Cana or Bávaro Beach make a good detour for fans of sun and sand. This route can be done in a day; those eager to visit and enjoy the eastern beaches should plan a night's stay.

BAYAHIBE AND THE ISLA SAONA

Follow the main road from La Romana in the direction of San Rafael de Yuma. After 8km (5 miles) the road crosses an impressive ravine, with the Río Chavón far below. Another 5km (3 miles) on, take the right turn to Bayahibe.

The town of ★**Bayahibe**, founded by Puerto Ricans, was once a quiet fishing village. Today it's a meeting-place for independent travellers, attracted by the great beach, cafés and restaurants and a choice of private accommodation, although the coast is dominated by all-inclusive resorts.

Map
on page
92

Star Attraction
● Bayahibe

Bringing home the catch

Map on page 92

Limited settlement

The largest settlement on Saona, Mano Juan, has a monument to the man who discovered the island: Jerónimo Anari. He is said to have landed here on 14 October 1495, named the island Bella Saona (after the Italian town of Savona), planted a tree, set up a cross and erected a gallows.

Bayahibe is the starting-point for the highly recommended excursion to the ★★ **Isla Saona** (117sq km/45sq miles, pop. 1,000). Catamarans or speedboats take visitors across to this island, which forms part of the Parque Nacional del Este. The boat trip passes untouched beaches and mangrove forests, finally reaching the island about two hours later.

There's nothing much to do on Isla Saona – except to enjoy some of the most pristine beaches in the Dominican Republic. One attraction is the *piscina natural*, a waist-deep lagoon surrounded by a sand bar, where you can stand and admire the white sand and palm trees.

SAN RAFAEL AND BOCA DE YUMA

Back on the main road, the next destination is **San Rafael de Yuma**. Just at the entrance to the town, a bumpy track leads off to the left, arriving 2km (1 mile) further on at the only sight this town has to offer: the **Casa Fuerte de Ponce de Léon**. It was from this fortress-like house that General Ponce de Léon, between 1505 and 1508, directed the conquest of the eastern part of the island and also founded Higüey. He left on his voyages to Puerto Rico and Florida from the nearby harbour of Boca de Yuma. The house still contains several interesting items of 16th-century furniture.

Laid-back Isla Saona

Roughly 10km (6 miles) to the east, ★ **Boca de Yuma** lies on a rock projecting into the ocean. The sea is rich in fish here. In June, deep-sea fishermen converge on this area to take part in an angling competition. There are several caverns along the rocky coast that can only be explored in the company of a guide.

Star Attraction
● Isla Saona

HIGUEY

Continue for another 48km (30 miles) from San Rafael de Yuma across flat grazing land to reach the provincial capital of **Higüey** (pop. 40,000), founded in the early 16th century. Soon afterwards it became a centre of pilgrimage when two Spanish soldiers brought a supposedly miracle-working painting of the Virgin Mary here. A church was built between 1512 and 1572 to house the picture (and then rebuilt in 1881 after destruction in an earthquake).

The Basílica de Nuestra Señora de la Altagracia.

Pilgrims have been visiting this church each year on 21 January since the late 17th century to commemorate the Spanish victory over the French at the battle of Limonada, fought on that day in 1691. The success is attributed to Nuestra Señora de Altagracia in Higüey, and she has been the country's official patron saint since 1922.

When the Old Cathedral in the town centre could no longer accommodate the vast number of pilgrims, the ★ **Basílica de Nuestra Señora de la Altagracia** was built nearby between 1952 and 1971. This mighty concrete structure, with its tower reminiscent of a jawbone, is entered through a door decorated with copper plate, bearing reliefs of the Miracle of Higüey. The statue of the virgin and a silver crown are in a glass case on the altar.

BEACH RESORTS

To the east of Higüey on the coast is a row of comfortable holiday resorts with attractive beaches; unfortunately they are very remote and even though the roads are good in this area there are no towns or villages to visit, or other sites of

Map on page 92

New town

In 2001 the Dominican government announced the construction of Pueblo Bávaro, a special new town to house the legions of workers employed at the Bávaro and Punta Cana tourist complexes. Situated close to the Punta Cana airport and served by a new aqueduct, the town is expected to attract some 40,000 people as the tourism industry in the country's southeast continues to expand.

A sheer-sided mogote *in Los Haïtises National Park*

interest nearby. The massive hotels include the **Bávaro Beach Resort** and the ★ **Punta Cana Beach Resort**.

Punta Cana and Bávaro are not towns as such, but rather purpose-built beachside tourist complexes, comprising all-inclusive hotels and associated restaurants and shops. The luxury resorts stretch for miles and even though no beach in the Dominican Republic can legally be deemed to be private, some of the hotels make public access to the sand extremely difficult.

All of these structures have been built since the 1980s and 1990s, sweeping away the few isolated fishing villages that previously occupied the idyllic beaches.

There is little room for Dominicans to make money out of tourists here, and local vendors are restricted to selling paintings and other handicraft on the beach. There are also bars and restaurants on the beaches, allowing tourists to escape their all-inclusive enclaves if they wish.

SABANA DE LA MAR

From Higüey the route continues westwards along the Carretera 4. The small town of **El Seibo**, rebuilt after the earthquake of 1751, is surrounded by cocoa and banana plantations. Another 24km (14 miles) to the west is **Hato Mayor**, a market town and provincial capital well-known for its cattle breeding (the name means 'large pasture'). Apart from its attractive park, the town has little to offer in the way of sights.

Carry on northwards from Hato Mayor on the Carretera 103 through a hilly tropical landscape. The rather dreary town of **Sabana de la Mar** lives off two things: the ferry traffic to and from Samaná *(see page 60)*, which finances several of the local restaurants and shops, and also the boat trips from here to the ★★ **Parque Nacional Los Haïtises** organised by the park administration. The excursions are to the coastal zone of the park, which covers an overall area of 208sq km (80sq miles). Inland, the dense mangrove jungle gradually turns into near-impenetrable tropical rainforest interspersed with limestone hillocks *(mogotes)*. Inside these rocky 'islands', huge caves, many as much as 300m (1,000ft) high, have been created by millions of years of rainfall. Some of these caverns contain paintings and rock carvings – evidence of Taíno habitation. Today the park is one of the most important reserves of flora and fauna in the country, with red, white and black mangroves and an array of birdlife including herons, pelicans and frigate birds.

Star Attraction
● **Parque Nacional Los Haïtises**

Below: Punta Cana coastline
Bottom: Bávaro Beach Resort

MICHES

The beach at Sabana de la Mar is not suitable for bathing; instead it's better to travel 40km (24 miles) further on along the badly-surfaced Carretera 104 to **Miches** (allow 90 minutes for the trip). The magnificent coast here is ideal for swimming and the beaches are often deserted.

The Reserva Científica Lagunas Redonda y Limón nature reserve (101sq km/39sq miles), a few miles east of Miches, is virtually inaccessible, and should be explored with the help of a guide. This unique bird sanctuary contains two lagoons that are just 1.5m (5ft) deep; the Laguna Redonda is the only one connected to the sea.

Travelling any further east along the coast from this point is not recommended, because of the poor condition of the roads.

A Diverse Heritage

Dominican culture represents an intermingling of various elements over the centuries – Indian, Spanish, African and American in particular. This mixture appears in various combinations across the Caribbean, and has resulted in a Creole culture with which many islanders happily identify.

Opposite: popular art depicting island life
Below: Taínos in wood, cigar store in Santo Domingo
Bottom: Taíno stone art

INDIAN INHERITANCE

The artistically and socially highly-developed Taíno Indian tribes were the cradle of Creole culture. Although they were almost completely exterminated a few decades after the arrival of the Spanish, elements of their culture lived on in local architecture, language and cuisine. Today *casabe* bread is still baked according to the Taíno recipe, and wooden houses are still built with thatched roofs and covered verandahs, based on the Indian *bohío* huts. Words like *tabaco* (tobacco), *huracán* (hurricane) and *canoa* (canoe) are all pre-Hispanic.

AFRICAN MEMORIES

African influence in the Republic is most strongly felt in San Pedro de Macorís, where the *gouloyas* – jesters playing cymbals and dressed in smocks adorned with mirrors – dance through the streets to the rhythmic accompaniment of African music. They symbolise the uprising of the slaves against their oppressors.

SPANISH INFLUENCE

Cultural life was strongly influenced by Spain. Literature and the arts largely reflected European styles. It was only from the mid-19th century onwards that any kind of 'national' style emerged. A Caribbean *modernismo* at the end of the 19th century was followed by relatively radical movements such as *postumismo*, which called all past artistic traditions into question and was related to the Dada movement in Europe, or *costumbrismo* which, though conventionally impressionistic in its formal language, insisted on the representation of Dominican themes alone. However, these attempts at cultural independence were repressed under the US occupation and the Trujillo regime.

Merengue – the National Music

From the moment you land in the Dominican Republic you are aware of having a constant companion: merengue, the music of the country. You will hear it on the radio in the taxi, at the hotel, in the bar, on the beach – everywhere. Dozens of small radio stations ensure that merengue is rarely out of earshot.

This fast music in 2/4 time and the dance of the same name (where the dancers hold each other closely and sway their hips a lot) emerged in the mid-19th century, when it developed as a local version of European dances for couples, such as *contredanse*. An Afro-Caribbean rhythm was added and the lyrics incorporated social commentary. It was popular with working people and despised by the upper classes, who continued to favour European dances.

Regional variations developed and a Haitian version, called *mereng* or *meringue*, spread across the border and influenced the Dominican merengue, to the disgust of the upper classes.

Traditionally a four-man combo played: the

Below: merengue music club
Bottom: merengue players in Las Terrenas

cuatro (guitar-like), *güira* (a cylindrical scraper of African origin), *tambora* (a double headed drum using male goatskin played with the hand on one head and female goatskin played with a stick on the other), and the *marimba* (an African-derived wooden box with plucked metal keys). By the 20th century the accordion had replaced the *cuatro* in the merengue bands around Santiago.

However, it was the dictator, Trujillo, who made it the national music. He popularised the *merengue típico* of the Cibao region around Santiago by commissioning bands to sing his praises. Brass and woodwind sections were added later, along with the electric keyboard and bass guitar. In the 1970s the dance steps became faster and less formal.

A typical merengue song starts with a short introduction, *paseo*, then the main part of the song, *merengue*, which is often social commentary, although contemporary tastes have led to bland love themes, followed by a call and response section, the *jaleo*.

To get an idea of just how enthusiastic the Dominicans are when it comes to music, observe Santo Domingo at the end of July and beginning of August each year. That's when the whole town celebrates its Merengue Festival, and the Malecón is transformed into one enormous open-air disco. There is also a merengue festival in Puerto Plata in October and another in Sosúa in September.

Alongside merengue there are several dances of African origin on the island, such as the *mangulina*, a circular dance, or the *carabine*, which originated during the struggle against the Haitians and is accompanied by a three-man band known as a *pripi*. Haitian music and dance has been imported by cane cutters, particularly *ra-ra*, the street celebration closely linked to voodoo (*vodú*). The Dominican version, *ga-gá*, is mostly heard along the border areas where voodoo is practised

Today's Cultural Variety

Following a phase of political consolidation in the 1960s and 1970s, art in the Dominican Republic is gradually reverting to African and Indian

> **Country music**
> The Dominican Republic's other famous home-grown musical style is *bachata*, a Caribbean equivalent of country and western, where the emphasis is on melodic ballads and poignant lyrics of broken hearts. Originally popular in rural areas and in the seedy dock areas and brothels, this music gained an international following when popularised by such stars as Juan Luis Guerra, Latin America's top-selling artist in the 1990s.

The rhythm section

roots. The Creole cultural movement known as *criollismo* is finding many adherents, especially in Santo Domingo.

In painting there has been a move towards connecting Indian symbolism with African colour and expressiveness. The epic literature reflects strong anti-American sentiment; it is clear that the Dominicans are loath to abandon their hard-won cultural identity. Controversial themes are no longer taboo. Women's role in a male-dominated society, the function of language and its dialects in self-realisation, the effects of increasing technology on community life, and the social conflict between rich and poor – all find reflection in art and literature. Creole culture is also becoming a lifestyle expression in its own right.

Below: US sporting influence
Bottom: Malecón parade

DOMINICANS AND THE US

Although a strain of anti-Yankee feeling remains detectable in literature, there is also a closer and more complex cultural relationship with the United States. Because of the large permanently settled Dominican population in and around New York, there is a constant intermingling of Caribbean and American influences in the work of younger Dominican artists and writers. Authors such as Julia Alvarez and Junot Díaz have written on the cultural disjuncture produced by having two homelands: *El Norte* (The North) and *La Isla* (The Island).

The tough lives lived by young Dominican-Americans or the culture shock experienced on returning to a small Dominican village make up some of the principal themes of these and other writers. A novel such as *How the Garcia Girls Lost Their Accents* by Julia Alvarez provides a wry look at how a middle-class Dominican family struggles to keep its identity in the melting-pot of New York.

Festivals and Folklore

Fun needs no official occasion here. In addition to the merengue festivals *(page 105)*, the majority of the population celebrates all the major

Catholic festivals, and the voodoo supporters *(see page 17)* celebrate their saints as well. On top of all that, however, there's carnival time.

CARNIVAL

The Dominicans are so passionate about carnivals that they have two: on **National Day** (27 February) and on **Restoration Day** (16 August). The carnival festivities were introduced by the Spanish but are also strongly influenced by African culture; the *diábolos*, or 'devils', who play an important role, are dressed differently in each region and wear very frightening masks. In Santo Domingo the devils are always played by men; in Santiago the *lechones* (devils with pigs' bladders tied around them) descend on the La Joya and Los Pepines suburbs; in Monte Cristi the *toros* (jesters dressed as bulls) tend to attack innocent passersby. The devils also chase evil spirits out of the island's cemeteries by cracking whips loudly.

The Cibao Valley town of La Vega can probably lay claim to the most enthusiastic Carnival celebrations in the country. Huge platoons of revellers, concealed by elaborate papier-mâché devil masks, roam the streets on every Sunday in February, while bands compete for prizes for the best Carnival songs. It is a huge, noisy affair, attracting some 50,000 spectators and participants.

> **Cockfighting**
> One very popular pursuit, especially in the smaller villages in rural areas, is cockfighting. Fights take place every Sunday in circular wooden arenas known as *gallería*. Every village has its Club Gallistico, or cockfighting club.

Carnival masks

FOOD AND DRINK

The local cuisine, *comida criolla*, has many roots; culinary traces have been left here not only by the Spanish colonisers but also by later immigrants and the tourist trade.

The Dominican equivalent of 'Montezuma's Revenge' is 'Caonabo's Revenge', and although Caonabo can sometimes strike, this should still not limit tourists to the luxury restaurants alone. As long as those with sensitive stomachs avoid eating unpeeled fruit and green salads, they can easily eat wherever the Dominicans eat – in a *restaurante criollo*, for instance, one of those small, tidy-looking restaurants where there's usually a choice of international as well as local specialities.

COMEDORES

It's cheaper and also even more 'Dominican' to eat in the so-called *comedores*. These simple restaurants can be found on every street corner, and as a rule there's no menu; instead, the dishes are presented inside a glass counter, which also makes ordering simple – all you have to do is point.

On trips into the interior, *paradas* are good places to eat. Located on most of the main routes, they're like *comedores*, only somewhat larger and more impersonal. Locals can often be seen peddling small and delicious snacks for travellers at many of the major traffic intersections and overland bus-stops: peeled oranges, sections of pineapple, peanuts, candy and highly colourful types of lemonade.

Snacks such as sandwiches, desserts (*dulces*) and drinks can be purchased in the numerous *cafeterías* and also in the *colmados*, grocery stores which seem to sell nearly everything and usually have a few chairs and tables handy.

A typical breakfast consists of sandwiches, fresh fruit and fried eggs. Dominicans tend to eat supper far later than Europeans. Classic main courses include *locrio*, a variant of paella allegedly invented by Spanish women when European ingredients were not available. The stew known as *sancocho* contains either chicken (*sancocho de pollo*) or various other kinds of meat (*sancocho prieto*). The ingredients, which can include maize, pumpkin and yam, tend to vary with the region and the cook involved.

The most popular dish is *bandera dominicana*, consisting of fried meat, beans and rice. It is usually accompanied by *tostones* or *fritos verdes* (strips of fried green banana) and salad. Some restaurants and many wayside snack bars sell marinated pieces of pork crackling (*chicharones*) or of chicken (*chicharones de pollo*), which make ideal snacks between meals.

LOCAL SPECIALITIES

Regional specialities are best tried out in the areas themselves. In Monte Cristi and Azua there's *chivo guisado*, goat stewed in a mixture of onions, rum and red wine; and the Samaná Peninsula produces the delicious *pescado con coco*, fish cooked in coconut milk sauce.

Exotic specials

Only the truly fearless visitor will want to sample *mondongo*, a national favourite of tripe stew, reputed both to cure hangovers and act as an aphrodisiac. A safer option is the similar sounding *mofongo*, a delicious mix of plantains, garlic and pork rinds. One local breakfast dish worth trying is *mangú*, nothing to do with mangoes but mashed plantains and onion drizzled with olive oil.

Although the Dominicans tend to favour meat over fish, seafood dishes are always available in the coastal areas. One speciality with allegedly aphrodisiac properties (though not for the squeamish) is *lambí* (conch).

The recipe for *casabe*, bread baked on a stone slab, dates back to the Taínos. *Yaniqueques*, pancakes fried in oil, were introduced by the *Cocolos*, the name given to immigrants from the English-speaking West Indian islands. Another absolutely delicious dessert is *coco nuevo con leche*, prepared from fresh coconut.

In the tropical heat, fruit juices *(jugos)* go a long way towards quenching thirst. The juice of various exotic fruits is usually freshly squeezed, or mixed with milk *(batida)*. *Refrescos* (lemonades) can be very strongly sweetened. Mountains of unripe green coconuts can often be seen at roadside vendors' stands. Their milk is known as *agua de coco* and is most refreshing.

NIGHTLIFE

Most hotels and resorts organise some sort of nocturnal activity, whether live music or discos. If you want to escape the tourist enclave and meet some Dominicans, then you'll find that every town has its choice of night spots, ranging from fly-blown *colmados* with little more than a fridge full of beer to high-tech discos playing local and American music.

> ### Sundowners
> Good drinks at sunset include *piña colada* (rum and pineapple juice), *batida de coco* (rum and coconut milk) and *daiquiri* (rum and lime juice). The most famous rum manufacturers are Barceló, Brugal, Bermúdez, Siboney and Macorix. The best quality rum is to be found in bottles bearing the words *añejo* (aged) or *Reserva Especial*.

In Santo Domingo the action doesn't really start until midnight. All of the big hotels in the capital have discos and casinos, ask at your hotel for recommendations. There are several bars and clubs in the city's fashionable colonial zone. Dress appropriately: nobody will be wearing shorts or T-shirts.

Single men can expect attention from professional 'hostesses', but a polite refusal will cause no offence. Similarly, single women will inevitably draw local admirers, but this is almost always harmless, if rather irritating. Go out in a group, if possible.

Discos tend to change names or close with astonishing regularity, so it's best to check details in the local press or English-language tourist publications.

WHAT TO DRINK

The most popular and also the most traditional alcoholic beverage on the island is, of course, rum *(ron)*. It can be drunk straight or on the rocks, or with Cola or Sprite – though whatever it gets mixed with, the proportion of rum is always alarmingly high.

Beer *(cerveza)* is served all over the Dominican Republic. Dominicans drink it cold, if not half frozen, and it is common for glasses to be stored in the freezer compartment for maximum chill factor. It's wise to check that your beer is not literally frozen by tipping it gently before opening the bottle.

Beer comes in three sizes – *pequeña* (small), *grande* (big) or 1 litre – and connoisseurs advise drinking the smaller version as it is less likely to lose its chill. It's common to see locals sharing a large bottle at a small corner store.

Some Dominicans prefer stronger varieties such as Quisqueya or Bohemia, but the best-selling brand by far is Presidente. It is ubiquitous, served in small village stores as well as luxury resort hotels. A classic European-style lager, Presidente was first brewed by German emigrants before the brewery evolved into one of the country's most profitable businesses, now part-owned by Guinness.

The beer owes its market dominance to a canny marketing ploy. The brewery offered bar- and shop-owners the large and efficient refrigerators that you will see throughout the country – on knock-down terms and on condition that they kept them filled with one specific brand. The plan seems to have worked, as Presidente rules the Dominican beer market.

Restaurant selection

The following suggestions from the Dominican Republic's main centres are listed according to three categories: $$$ = expensive; $$ = moderate; $ = inexpensive.

Barahona
Brisas del Caribe, Malecón, tel: 809 524 2794. Very good fish and seafood served on a pleasant patio. $
La Rocca, Malecón, tel: 809 524 4918. Good value local Dominican dishes, especially breakfast. $

Bávaro
Capitán Cook, Playa Cortecito, tel: 809 552 0646. In a shady spot on the beach, popular with people escaping all-inclusive hotel fare. Fresh lobster, fish, shrimp, or steak. Wash it down with a jug of sangria. $$

Cabarete
Casa del Pescador, tel: 809 571 0760. Excellent seafood on the beach. $$
Lax, on the beach. No phone. The place is always lively with Mexican, sushi or international dishes on the menu. Meeting place for windsurfers. $

Jarabacoa
La Herradura, Independencia, corner with Duarte. Varied menu; ranch- style décor. Live music some nights. $
Rancho Restaurant, opposite Esso station. Good food and artistic ambiance. $

Las Terrenas
Casa Boga, Pueblo de los Pescadores, tel: 809 240 6321. Basque-run place; the best seafood right on the sand. $$
Dinny, on the beach. Very good local food all day, especially breakfast. $
La Salsa, Pueblo de los Pescadores at the beach, tel: 809 240 6805. French-run restaurant with beautiful terrace overlooking the sea. $$

Fish restaurant,
Playa Grande, Río San Juan

Monte Cristi
El Bistro, San Fernando 26, tel: 809 579 2021. Courtyard dining. Local specialities, goat, lobster, pasta. $

Puerto Plata
Aguaceros, Malecón, near the old fire station, tel: 809 586 2796. Bar and restaurant with alfresco dining. Mexican dishes, steaks and burgers. $
La Parrillada Steak House, Manolo Tavarez Justo, tel: 809 586 1401. With outdoor seating; Argentine steak and hearty helpings. $$

Samaná
Café de Paris, Malecón, tel: 809 538 2488. Pizza and crêpes; cocktails in the evening. $
L'Hacienda, Malecón, tel: 809 538 2383. Famous for its succulent kebabs and barbecues. $$

Santiago de los Caballeros
Pez Dorado, Calle del Sol 43, tel: 809 582 2518. Best Creole and international food in town. $$
El Café, Avenida Texas, Los Jardines, tel: 809 587 4247. Small restaurant, with excellent international cuisine. $$
Ciao Ciao, Los Jardines, tel: 809 583 1092. Italian-owned pasta and pizza restaurant. $$

Santo Domingo
Ananda, Casimiro de Moya, tel: 809 682 7153. One of the best vegetarian restaurants in town. $
La Briciola, Arzobispo Meriño 152, tel: 809 688 5055. Excellent food in a colonial setting. $$$
El Conde de Peñalba, Plaza Colón, tel: 809 688 7121. Inexpensive lunch in the heart of the capital. $
El Conuco, Casimiro de Moya, tel: 809 686 0129. Traditional Dominican cooking in rustic ambience. $$
Fogaraté, Avenida George Washington 517, tel: 809 686 0044. Dominican specialities under a thatched roof. $$
Fonda La Atarazana, Calle Atarazana 5, tel: 809 689 2900. Fine Dominican cuisine. $$$
Mesón de Bari, Calle Hostos, junction Salome Ureña. Local haunt of academics and artists, where simple but delicious dishes are served until 9pm. $
Mesón de la Cava, in a natural cave in Mirador del Sur Park, tel: 809 533 2818. Creole cuisine, dancing. $$$
Palacio del Mofongo, George Washington 509, tel: 809 688 8121. The place to try Dominican specialities. $$
Pat'e Palo, Calle Atarazana 25, tel: 809 687 8089. Waiters dressed as pirates serve good French-Italian food. $$$
Sully, Charles Summers y Calle Caoba, tel: 809 562 3389. Excellent seafood some distance from centre. $$$
Vesuvio Pizzeria, Malecón 523. Child-friendly and informal, serving pasta and pizzas to families. $

Sosúa
El Atlántico, in Los Charamicos. Cliffside; romantic atmosphere. $$
On the Waterfront, El Batey, tel: 809 571 3024. Fish and seafood with a fine view over the sea. $$
La Puntilla, tel: 809 571 2215. Sea view from the former summer home of an American diplomat. $$
La Roca, Pedro Clisante, tel: 809 571 3893. Fish, seafood and shrimp sold by the pound. Mexican and pasta. $$

Drinking local style

If you're going for an alcoholic night out, the cheapest way of buying drinks is the local method: order a *servicio:* a bottle of rum, a handful of mixers and a large bucket of ice. This is easier and more economical than ordering single drinks. In some bars and discos this is known as a *servicio Cuba Libre* and the mixer provided will automatically be Coke.

ACTIVE HOLIDAYS

Fine white sand, turquoise sea, soft green palm trees and not a cloud in the sky – like most islands in the Antilles, the Dominican Republic is ideal for all kinds of sporting pursuits, on the land as well as in and on the water. The hotels in the larger beach resorts all offer numerous opportunities to practise or to learn sports, and if they don't do exactly what's required they will be able to provide the address of somewhere that does.

DIVING

The astonishingly colourful and varied undersea flora and fauna isn't the only attraction for divers: there are also something in the region of 400 wrecked ships lying off the coast of Hispaniola, some of them five centuries old, plus lots of lost anchors and cannons – it's a veritable underwater museum.

The south of the island is better for diving because the Caribbean tends to be calmer than the Atlantic, with its sharp winds, though local professional divers have their favourite areas on both the north and the south coasts.

In the Parque Submarino La Caleta, around 20km (12 miles) east of Santo Domingo, a wrecked ship has been sunk to create an artificial reef. La Caleta is considered a first-class diving ground and has coral, sponges and several very colourful species of fish.

To the west of the capital, divers should try the area around the delta of the Río Haina, where salt and freshwater mix, as well as the coast off Palenque where there is a wrecked ship dating from 1806. The still relatively unexplored reefs and caves around the Isla Beata are home to numerous fascinating examples of undersea flora and fauna.

In the north, the enormous coral reef known as Silver Banks, 140km (87 miles) to the northeast of Puerto Plata, and also the Bay of Samaná are both excellent destinations for divers.

For more information contact: Actividades Acuáticas in Santo Domingo (tel: 809 688 5838) or Boca Chica (tel: 809 523 4511).

There are good diving schools in almost all of the larger tourist resorts (e.g. Northern Coast Aquasports in Sosúa, Gri Gri Divers in San Juan or Scubafun in Bayahibe).

Horse-riding on the beach is popular

WINDSURFING AND KITE SURFING

The very best place for windsurfers and kite surfers is the village of Cabarete on the north coast. The small bay is protected by a reef, and the wind and wave conditions here are held in high regard by the world's top professionals. For beginners, there are more than a dozen schools to choose from.

DEEP-SEA FISHING

Fishing competitions are held annually, the catch being blue marlin, bonito and dorado. In June, a competition is staged near Boca de Yuma, the most popular deep-sea fishing area. For more information contact the nearest Club Náutico (for the club in Santo Domingo, tel: 809 566 1682).

RIVER SPORTS

The exciting sports of whitewater rafting, kayaking, canyoning, cascading and tubing are all available on the mountain rivers of the Baiguate, the Jimenoa and Yaque del Norte, within easy reach of Jarabacoa. The best time to shoot the rapids is after the rain, when the rivers are flowing fast. Companies operating in Jarabacoa: Aventuras del Caribe, at Rancho Jarabacoa (tel: 809 242 0395) and Máxima Aventura, at Rancho Baiguate (tel: 809 574 6890).

GOLF

There are more than two dozen golf courses on the north and east coasts. All the large resort hotels around the coast have at least one, and most are of championship standard. The luxurious Casa de Campo, near La Romana, has three 18-hole courses. One of the courses, known as the 'Teeth of the Dog', is believed to be among the best in the world. There are other well-established courses at Playa Grande, near Río San Juan, which follow the coastline. At Playa Dorada, near Puerto Plata, there is a par 72 course.

There are several courses in the far east at Punta Cana and Playa Bávaro, and also around Santo Domingo and Santiago. There are a few 9-hole courses, including one in Jarabacoa and another at Samaná.

RIDING AND POLO

Many hotels provide horses for riding into the surrounding area. The most common local breed is called *Paso Fino*, or 'gentle step', and they really are easy to ride.

The Casa de Campo Hotel has several polo fields. You can watch games during the season (November to May) and lessons are offered as well.

Those keen on betting can try their luck at the Hipódromo Quinto Centenario racetrack near Santo Domingo.

HIKING AND MOUNTAINEERING

The hiking centre of the Dominican Republic is Jarabacoa, located in the Central Highlands. With their year-round spring temperatures, the pine forests are marvellously refreshing places to hike.

Climbing the highest peak in the Caribbean, the Pico Duarte (3,087m/10,128ft) at the southern edge of the Armando Bermúdez National Park, is worth the effort. An excursion like this is best organised via Rancho Baiguate in Jarabacoa, tel: 809 574 6890, or Iguana Mama in Cabarete, tel: 809 571 0908, who will provide experienced guides and the necessary park permits.

On two wheels

Cycling is a great way to see remote areas of the country, even if extreme caution is required with regard to motorists and potholes. Mountain bikes can be rented from Iguana Mama in Cabarete, tel: 809 571 0908, a company that also organises hiking and biking tours and white water rafting.

PRACTICAL INFORMATION

Getting There

BY AIR

The Dominican Republic is served by the major American, European and Latin American airlines, and a number of Caribbean-island operators.

There are international airports at Santo Domingo (south coast), Puerto Plata (north coast), Punta Cana (east coast) and La Romana (southeast coast). An airport tax of US$20 has to be paid on departure from the country.

From Europe

Several airlines have scheduled services to the Dominican Republic, usually with onward or connecting flights. They include:

Air France (daily from London via Paris), tel: 0845 084 5111; www.airfrance.com

American Airlines (daily from London via New York or Miami), tel: 0845 778 9789.

Iberia (daily via Madrid, 4 times a week with a stopover in Puerto Rico), tel: 0845 601 2854; www.iberia.com

Other airlines include Air Europa and Air Madrid from Madrid, Lauda Air from Milan, Martinair from Amsterdam, Condor and LTU from selected German cities.

The Dominican Republic is an increasingly popular charter destination. See your local travel agent for details about package holidays which usually include flights, airport transfers and accommodation.

From North America

American Airlines (daily direct flights from Boston, New York and Miami), tel: 800-433 7300; www.aa.com

Continental (daily from New York), tel: 800-231 0856; www.continental.com

Other carriers include US Airways, Delta and the budget airlines JetBlue and Spirit Airlines. Air Canada also flies from several Canadian cities.

There is also a good choice of charter operators that run services to the Dominican Republic.

From the Caribbean

American Eagle (tel: 800-433 7300; www.aa.com) flies to Santo Domingo from St Thomas, USVI, and St Maarten, and to Puerto Plata and Punta Cana from San Juan, Puerto Rico. Alternative Caribbean airlines include BWIA and Air Jamaica.

Buses link the main towns.
It's best to book seats in advance

BY SEA

There are cargo and passenger shipping services operating from New York, New Orleans, Miami and South American countries. Several cruise lines from the US, Canada and Europe include the Dominican Republic on their itineraries. Details from the Republic's tourist offices in the country concerned.

Getting Around

BY CAR AND MOTORBIKE

The main north-south route, the Autopista Duarte, from Santo Domingo to Santiago, is a motorway; the other main roads along the north and south coasts are also well surfaced. The road along the south coast out to the eastern beach resorts is being improved to provide a motorway link. In other parts of the country, and especially on side roads, potholes and other surface damage have to be reckoned with.

Routes which look quite important on maps often turn out to be nothing more than bumpy dirt tracks that are sometimes closed depending on the season. This is particularly true of the interior. Ask the locals which route they would recommend.

Motoconchos, the cheapest way to get around

Speed checks

Hire cars are often a target for police, who claim that they have been speeding. There are three options: pay a small 'fine' ($10 is normally enough); protest firmly but politely, in which case the policeman may become bored and give up; ignore the waving officer and drive by – this is what most worldly-wise Dominicans do. If you choose the last option, it's best not to return by the same route too quickly.

Signposting is poor and you may have to ask the way as you go. Animals wandering about or lying in the road are another hazard.

Near police stations, schools, barracks, at the entrance and exit of all towns and at intersections in towns and villages, look out for the *policía acostado* (road humps or 'sleeping policemen'). They can appear abruptly and not even the locals always spot them in time. You need to be vigilant.

The maximum speed allowed is 80kmph (50mph). Watch out in the larger towns: Dominican drivers tend to behave with complete disregard for the highway code, changing lanes without indicating (indicators are often missing), riding mopeds down one-way streets in the wrong direction, slamming on the

brakes of their minibuses if they spot their passengers too late, etc. Drivers from abroad would be advised to travel with caution and always stay alert. Eye contact is the best communication. Travelling by night should be avoided.

Hire Cars and Motorbikes

The main car rental firms have offices at the major airports and in the larger towns and tourist centres. You usually have to provide a driver's license and a credit card, and you'll need to pay a large deposit. Be sure to ask about insurance regulations, otherwise things can become very expensive if an accident does occur.

Hiring motorbikes and mopeds is a risky business. Many rental firms won't insure you. In the tourist centres, bikes and mopeds are a popular target for thieves. Drivers are required to wear a helmet.

BY AIR

Air Santo Domingo offers scheduled air connections to popular tourist destinations within the Dominican Republic several times daily. For further information, tel: 809 683 8006.

BY BUS

The main towns are easily reached by bus. Buses in the Dominican Republic are comfortable and many of them have air-conditioning, too. The three largest bus companies are Metro, Caribe Tours and Terrabús. Visitors are recommended to reserve seats in advance.

BY GUAGUA

On lesser roads, smaller buses known as *guaguas* are more common. These can be boarded in the central square of most villages, or hailed with a wave from the roadside. The problem is, most *guaguas* are jam-packed with passengers. Considered in a positive light, it's a great way of meeting people.

BY PICK-UP

Another form of transportation is the pick-up truck; passengers simply sit in the open back.

BY PUBLICOS AND MOTOCONCHOS

The *carros públicos* (or *conchos*), cars or minibuses that function as shared taxis, can be found in all the larger towns. To get a ride, just stand at the roadside and signal to the driver. The *públicos* travel along fixed routes, but if you are unfamiliar with the area you should always check them with a map first.

The cheapest form of motorised transportation, very much in evidence on the north coast, are the mopeds or *motoconchos*. It's not uncommon to see up to three or even four people plus the rider sitting on these. Decide on the fare in advance.

BY TAXI

Taxis are far more expensive than *públicos*. The half-hour trip from the airport to the centre of Santo Domingo costs US$20–30.

It is always possible to hire a taxi, complete with driver, for a half or full day. This is a good way of seeing some of the less accessible sights and avoiding harassment in tourist spots. Always negotiate a price beforehand, and remember that your driver will expect to be bought lunch and/or drinks.

> **Unfair fares**
> Remember that taxi and *motoconcho* fares are likely to rise steeply at night. There are never meters in taxis, and some unscrupulous drivers have been known to quote a price in pesos and then claim that they meant dollars. It can be easier to pay before setting off to avoid any such misunderstanding, genuine or not.

Facts for the Visitor

TRAVEL DOCUMENTS

Visitors from most European countries, as well as from the US, Canada and Australia, do not require a visa to enter the Dominican Republic. Nationals of Canada and the USA only need appropriate ID such as a birth certificate and a driver's licence which proves citizenship; for UK nationals a passport valid for at least six months is necessary.

All visitors who enter the country are required to purchase a tourist card *(tarjeta del tourista)* which costs US$10. This is very often included with the airline ticket, otherwise it can be obtained at the airport or at the border crossings. The card allows tourists to remain in the country for a maximum of 90 days (single entry), and a small financial penalty is imposed on individuals who extend their visit beyond this period. For an extension of residency or stay, the Department of Immigration can be reached at tel: 809 685 2535.

CUSTOMS REGULATIONS

Visitors to the Dominican Republic are allowed to bring in 2 litres of alcohol, 200 cigarettes and gift articles not exceeding the value of US$1,000. If you are travelling with any expensive cameras, computers or personal stereos, make sure you convince the customs officers that they are for your own personal use and will be taken with you when you leave. If you ask the officials to make a note of the equipment in your passport there should be no problem. Your reception may depend on where your flight is coming from and the attitude of the inspector, but usually he or she will let you through with a smile. The airport police are on the lookout for illegal drugs. It is also illegal to bring firearms into the country.

TOURIST INFORMATION
In the US
Dominican Republic Tourist Board, 136 E 57th Street, Suite 803, New York, NY 10022, tel: 212-588 1012, fax: 212-588 1015, e-mail: newyork@sectur.gov.do
248 NW Le Jeune Road, Miami, Florida 33126, tel: 305-444 4592, fax: 305-444 4845, e-mail: miami@sectur.gov.do

In the UK
Dominican Republic Tourist Board, 18–20 Hand Court, High Holborn, London WC1V 6JF, tel: 020 7242 7778, fax: 020 7405 4202, e-mail: inglaterra@sectur.gov.do.

In the Dominican Republic
Secretaria de Estado de Turismo (Department of Tourism), Avenida México, Santo Domingo, tel: 809 221 4660, 1-200-3500 (toll-free in Dominican Republic), fax: 809 682 3806. Puerto Plata, tel: 809 586 3676.
Dirección Nacional de Parques (National Park Administration), Avenida Máximo Gómez, La Cementera, Santo Domingo, tel: 1-809 472 4204, fax: 809 472 4012.

RECOMMENDED WEBSITES

The Dominican Republic Tourist Board website is www.dominicanrepublic.com; visitors are also recommended to try the following: www.drhotels.com, www.hispaniola.com, www.drpure.com and www.dr1.com.

AIRLINE OFFICES IN SANTO DOMINGO

Air France, Avenida Máximo Gómez 15, Plaza el Faro, tel: 809 686 8432.
American Airlines: Edificio In Tempo, 4th floor, Avenida Winston Churchill, tel: 809 542 5151.
American Eagle (subsidiary of American Airlines with flights to San Juan, Puerto Rico), Edificio In Tempo, Avenida Winston Churchill, tel: 809 542 5151.

Continental, Edificio In Tempo, Suite 104, Avenida Winston Churchill, tel: 809 562 6688.
Iberia, Avenida Lopez de Vega 63, Edificio J/J Roca 2nd Floor, tel: 809 508 0188.
Lufthansa, Avenida George Washington 353, tel: 809 689 9625.

Cash machines
Automated teller machines (ATMs) are to be found in Santo Domingo and most towns and will provide cash against your debit and credit cards. Instructions are usually in English as well as Spanish.

CURRENCY AND EXCHANGE

The official unit of currency in the Dominican Republic is the peso (RD$), divided into 100 centavos. There are 5, 10, 20, 50, 100, 500 and 1,000 peso banknotes, and it's always best to have a few 5 and 10 peso notes handy for excursions and *guagua* rides *(see page 117)*, because larger notes can't usually be changed.

It is best to take US dollars in cash or as traveller's cheques, because exchanging them is no problem. MasterCard, Visa and American Express are the most commonly accepted credit cards. Visitors are advised to exchange money at banks because that's where you will get the best rate, otherwise make use of your hotel's foreign exchange facility. Be advised that black market transactions are illegal. Beware of confidence tricksters.

Import or export of the local currency is forbidden. However, there is no limit on the amount of foreign currency that can be brought into the Dominican Republic.

OPENING TIMES
Banks
8.30am–3pm, Monday to Friday.
Shops
8am–7pm, Monday to Friday. Some shops are open on Saturday and Sunday morning.
Post offices
8am–5pm, Monday to Saturday.
Government offices
7.30am–2.30pm, Monday to Friday.
Private offices (and some shops)
8.30am–12.30pm and 2.30–6.30pm, Monday to Friday.
Museums and places of interest
Closed Monday. The official opening times aren't always precise, and are often subject to change at short notice for no apparent reason.

Change money in banks or hotels

PUBLIC HOLIDAYS

1 January (New Year's Day)
6 January (Epiphany)
21 January (Festival of Our Lady of Altagracia, the country's patron saint)
26 January (*Día de Duarte*, the birthday of Juan P. Duarte, the founder of the Republic)
27 February (*Día de la Independencia*, National Independence Day)
March–April (*Semana Santa*, Good Friday and Easter Sunday)
1 May (Labour Day)
May (Ascension, Corpus Christi)
15 August (Assumption of the Virgin)
16 August (Restoration Day)
24 September (Day of Patron Saint Nuestra Señora de las Mercedes)
12 October (*Día de la Raza*, Columbus Day)
25 December (Christmas Day)

POSTAL SERVICES

The postal service is very slow. It is best not to put your mail in the rather unreliable post boxes, but to pay a little extra for *entrega especial* (special delivery), for which post offices have a separate window.

TELEPHONE

The international dialling code for the Dominican Republic is 809. The country has a modern telecommunications network. Public payphones are commonplace in towns and cities; many of them now take phone cards, which you can buy from general stores and newsagents. However, for international calls it's best to use a call centre. The two main phone companies are Verizon and Tricom. When using a call centre, dial the number you want and an operator will ask for the name of the party you require plus the number of the booth you're in (in Spanish or in English). You pay when you leave (credit cards are accepted).

If you are calling from one place to another on the island, always dial 1 before the number. For the UK dial 011 44, followed by the area code (minus its initial zero) and then the number itself. Phone numbers in the Dominican Republic all have 10 digits and begin with 809, which is also the international dialling code. International access codes are, MCI: 1-800 888 8000; Sprint: 1-800 751 7877; AT&T: 1-800 872 2881.

NEWSPAPERS, RADIO, TELEVISION

Several Spanish-language newspapers provide up-to-date information: *Listín Diario, El Caribe, Hoy* and *Diario Libre* in the morning; *Ultima Hora* and *El Nacional* in the afternoon; and *Primicias* on Sunday. *Touring* is a multilingual tourist newspaper.

The Dominican Republic has nearly 200 radio stations and 7 television channels. Most hotels can receive American cable TV.

CLOTHING

Neatness is very important to the Dominicans. Even the poorest will invest much of the little they have in looking presentable. Any tourist who walks through the streets wearing flip-flops, tight swimming trunks and a scanty T-shirt is considered stupid, and offends the aesthetic sense of the locals. Swimming things should be kept close to the beach. At other times it's best to wear light clothing made of

> ### Tipping
> In hotels a 22 percent surcharge is levied on the basic price, composed of 12 percent tax for the room and 10 percent for service. An additional 12 percent tax is also charged on meals in restaurants, plus another 10 percent service charge. However, it's still customary to express your satisfaction by leaving a 5–10 percent gratuity as well.

cotton or other natural fibres; take a sweater for cooler evenings and rainwear in case of tropical downpours. For hikes in the mountains and national parks, sturdy footwear is essential.

TIME ZONES

The Dominican Republic has Atlantic Standard Time (AST), which is Central European Time minus five hours. During European summer time the difference is six hours.

VOLTAGE

The voltage in the Dominican Republic is 110v, and the sockets fit American plugs. There are quite a few power cuts (*apagones*), especially in the evenings when consumption is high. Many hotels have their own generators (*plantas*) to handle the situation. It could well prove useful, however, to carry a torch and/or a candle in your luggage.

SOUVENIRS

Shopping in the Dominican Republic is most appreciated by people who don't mind haggling. The locals are experts at this. The most popular purchases include jewellery made of amber, *larimar* (a turquoise-coloured gemstone unique to the Dominican Republic), gold or silver.

One of the opening scenes of Steven Spielberg's *Jurassic Park* was set in the Dominican Republic and shows a 100-million-year-old insect found trapped in amber in a quarry. A tiny drop of dinosaur blood from its stomach provided enough DNA information for scientists to bring dinosaurs back to life... Well, the Dominican Republic does indeed have rich supplies of amber – that much is true. It's a fossil tree resin that occurs in all shades of yellow with nuances of orange and brown. Deeply coloured transparent amber is highly prized as gem material and is used to make necklaces,

rings and bracelets. The leaves, ants or spiders it sometimes contains, often several million years old, provide fascinating information on the way the earth's flora and fauna have evolved.

Beware not to purchase articles made of black coral or tortoiseshell, for ecological reasons as well as your own safety: trading in or exporting these materials is strictly forbidden, as is importing them to the US and most European countries.

It's impossible to miss the colourful paintings in all shapes and sizes exhibited by Haitians in all the tourist areas. Wickerwork, leather goods, wood carvings, machetes, carnival masks and the famous *muñeca sin rostro* (faceless clay dolls) from the region around Moca are good buys.

Hand-rolled cigars also make traditional souvenirs.

MEDICAL

Vaccinations recommended to visitors to the tropical Caribbean islands are against Hepatitis A and B. Your polio and tetanus shots should also be up to date. Malaria precautions are not generally required unless you are planning to spend some time in the border

Insect pests

The cockroaches (*cucarachas*) can sometimes be as long as a human finger; they may look disgusting, but they're not at all dangerous to humans. The mosquitoes are another story: they can be troublesome during the evening, despite the people with spray devices who rush round the tourist hotels. Even worse than mosquitoes are the buffalo gnats (*jejenes*) that hover close to the ground. Fly sprays are only of limited use here, so wear trousers, socks and a long-sleeved shirt when dusk falls. In some areas, a mosquito net (*mosquitero*) will come in handy; they're available on request from every hotel.

region close to Haiti. However there was an outbreak of malaria in 2004, in the east of the country.

Another mosquito-borne disease, dengue fever, is also prevalent so use of mosquito repellent is essential.

The best way to prevent any stomach or bowel complaints is to drink only pure water *(agua purificada)*, sold in plastic bottles. Ice cubes, ice cream, fresh salads and fruit juices are often prepared using pure water, but if in doubt they should be avoided.

It's best to take out some kind of health insurance before going to the Dominican Republic. Make sure transportation back home is also included in the cover in case of severe illness.

The health system in the Dominican Republic is adequate. Most towns have their own doctors and clinics, and tourist centres always do. Payment has to be made immediately following treatment; receipts are provided. Down-payments have to be made for hospital stays.

CRIME

Many people have a false impression of crime levels in developing countries. The crime rate in the Dominican Republic is far lower than that of most European countries, and outside

Accidents can happen

Photography

Photographic material, especially slide film, can be purchased only in the larger tourist centres or in hotel sthops, and is often overpriced. Dominicans generally don't mind having their photographs taken, but it's best to ask first.

the tourist centres it's relatively safe. The main holiday centres have to cope with prostitution, drug smuggling and black marketeering. Keep an eye on your documents and personal possessions and avoid obviously dangerous situations (e.g. remote beaches at dusk, shady bars and neighbourhoods). The larger hotels have a safe for valuables. Never leave your luggage or any valuables in your rental car.

EMERGENCIES

For ambulance, police and the fire department, dial 911.

DIPLOMATIC REPRESENTATION

US Embassy and Consulate, Avenida César Nicolás Pensón, Santo Domingo, tel: 809 221 2171.
British Embassy and Consulate, Avenida 27 de Febrero 233, Building Corominas Pepín, Santo Domingo, tel: 809 472 7111; fax: 809 472 7190.

ACCOMMODATION

The Dominican Republic has various types of accommodation: tourist hotels conform to international standards, come in various price categories and often have their own restaurant or nightclub attached; apart-hotels have self-catering facilities and are useful for longer stays; boarding houses range from spartan to very comfortable, and so does the service. Boarding houses are the cheapest accommodation, though prices for the simplest rooms fluctuate wildly depending on the region.

In the Dominican Republic itself, information on accommodation can be obtained from Tourist Information at Santo Domingo International Airport, and there is also an information office on the Malecón in Puerto Plata. For descriptions of accommodation, it's worth looking at the English-language newspaper *Touring*; another good source of information is the website www.drhotels.com

Only the very courageous – who don't mind a disappointment – would be advised to follow the people who can sometimes be seen hanging round the airport waving colour photographs of 'exclusive bungalows right next to the sea'; somehow, the photos don't always accurately reflect the reality.

The best way to find accommoda-tion in the smaller resorts is to sit in one of the cafés and simply ask the locals or the tourists there. By the way, a word of warning: motels very often turn out to be short stay places for courting couples.

HOTEL SELECTION

The following suggestions from the main centres are listed according to three categories: $$$ = expensive; $$ = moderate; $ = inexpensive.

Baní

Hotel Salinas, Puerto Hermoso 7 (16km/10 miles out of Baní), tel: 809 346 8855. Windsurfers' and fisher-men's base on saltflats, but a pleas-ant hotel with good restaurant and pool. $$

Barahona

Barceló Bahoruco Beach Resort, Baoruco, tel: 809 524 1111. Large all-inclusive resort with 105 rooms in modern blocks around the pool and overlooking a stony beach with rough waves. $$$

Casa Bonita, Baoruco, Carretera de la Costa Km16, tel: 809 696 0215. Stylish and quiet hotel with great views and good food. $$

Caribe, Avenida Enriquillo, tel: 809 524 4111. Basic and noisy. $

Bávaro

Barceló Bávaro Beach Resort, tel: 809 686 5797. Vast complex of five resorts, over 2000 rooms and a town in itself. $$

Cortecito Inn, Playa Cortecito, tel: 809 552 0639. Over the road from the beach, near the Capitán Cook restau-rant. One of the few hotels here that isn't all-inclusive. Large, simple rooms around a garden and pool. $$

> **Self-catering**
> Aparthotels are sometimes a con-venient and economical option for families who would prefer not to stay in all-inclusive establishments or eat out every evening. Most are equipped with basic kitchen equipment, and it can be fun to go and buy food at corner shops and local mar-kets rather than in US-style supermarkets.

Bayahibe

Hotel Bayahibe, on the main street, tel: 809 833 0159. Excellent budget option and convenient for the dive shops and the beach. **$**

Villa Iguana, tel: 809 833 0203. German run and centrally located, with dive packages and excursions available. Smart and good value. **$$**

Boca Chica

Calypso Beach Hotel, 20 de Diciembre, tel: 809 523 4666. Near beach, modern and friendly. **$**

Coral Hamaca, Calle Duarte, tel: 809 523 4611. Large resort hotel with all amenities. **$$$**

Don Juan Beach Resort, tel: 809 523 4511. On the beach but also in the middle of town. **$$$**

> **Playing safe**
> It is worth paying a little extra to hire a safe in your room when it is available. Thefts do occur, even in the best establishments, and a safe will protect your money, credit cards and passports.

Cabarete

Caracol, tel: 809 571 0680. On the beach at the western end of the village. Studios or apartments; lots of activities and good for families or sporting enthusiasts. **$$**

Kitebeach, tel: 809 571 0878. Perfect for kite surfers with packages and lessons, storage of gear and other facilities. A variety of rooms, from budget to superior, or apartments. **$$**

Palm Beach Condos, tel: 809 571 0758. Centrally situated by the beach but quiet and pleasant. **$$**

Residencia Dominicana, tel: 809 571 0890. Great value studios or apartments with pool, tennis and a restaurant. **$**

Velero Beach Resort, Calle La Punta 1, tel: 809 571 9727. Comfortable hotel at the end of the beach with rooms and suites which can be combined to create spacious, luxury apartments. **$$**

Constanza

Cabañas de la Montaña, tel: 809 539 3268. Self-contained villas with cooking facilities; wonderful views. **$**

Jarabacoa

Gran Jimenoa, Avenida La Confluencia, Los Corralitos, tel: 809 574 6304. Out of town along the Jimenoa River at a wonderful location. Very popular with Dominicans at weekends. Good local food. **$**

Rancho Baiguate, tel: 809 574 4940. Comfortable accommodation in an idyllic mountain setting, and a good base for walking and horse riding. **$$**

Juan Dolio

Barceló Capella Beach Resort, tel: 809 526 1080. Excellent beach hotel with pleasant rooms and grounds. **$$**

Barceló Colonia Tropical, tel: 809 526 1660. Not all-inclusive and smaller than most others here. **$$**

Coral Costa Caribe, tel: 809 526 2244. A large all-inclusive resort with standard amenities and entertainment for guests. **$$**

Talanquera Beach Resort, tel: 809 526 1510. Huge complex with all facilities. **$$$**

La Romana

Casa de Campo, tel: 809 523 3333. Exclusive complex, complete with golf course and all amenities. **$$$**

Olimpo, tel: 809 550 7646. Simple but friendly hotel. **$**

Las Terrenas

Acaya, Playa Bonita, tel: 809 240 6161. Good food and a pleasant location. **$**

Atlantis, Playa Bonita, tel: 809 240 6111. French-run with good food. **$$**

Coyamar, Playa Bonita, tel: 809 248 2353. This German-run hotel has a friendly atmosphere. **$**
El Portillo Beach Club, tel: 809 688 5717. Many beach activities for all-inclusive package tourists. **$$**
Tropic Banana, tel: 809 240 6110. Popular hotel with good restaurant and lively bar. **$**

Luperón
Luperon Beach Resort, Ciudad Marina, tel: 809 571 8303. Lots of variety in facilities. **$$**

Miches
La Loma, tel: 809 558 5564. On a hilltop overlooking the coast. Simple rooms with balcony views. Restaurant, but a poor road leads to the hotel. **$**

Monte Cristi
Chic, Benito Monción 44, tel: 809 579 2316. Old-fashioned and friendly. **$**

Puerto Plata
Aparta-Hotel Lomar, Malecón 8, tel: 809 320 8555. Small hotel with large rooms, some with balcony overlooking the sea. **$**
El Indio, Plaza Anacaona, 30 de Marzo 94–8, tel: 809 586 1201. Clean and good value with a restaurant. **$**
Gran Ventana Beach Club, Playa Dorada, tel: 809 320 2111. All inclusive holiday village at the beach. **$$$**
Victoria Resort, Playa Dorada, tel: 809 320 1200. Standard all-inclusive set-up by the golf course. **$$$**

Punta Cana
Club Mediterranée, tel: 809 567 5228. All possible beach and sports facilities, with activities for children. **$$$**
Punta Cana Beach Resort, tel: 809 687 2503. Large all-inclusive, with golf course, beach and watersports, but rather isolated. **$$**

Río San Juan
Bahía Blanca, Gastón Deligne 5, tel: 809 589 2528. The hotel has a lovely situation on cliffs overlooking the sea, and the beach is close by. Quiet and peaceful. **$**

Samaná
Bahía View, Avenida Circunvalación 4, tel: 809 538 2186. Small conveniently located hotel with a view of the bay; 10 rooms all with different decor. Restaurant on the first floor. **$**
Gran Bahía, tel: 809 538 3111. Luxury all-inclusive resort outside town, with beautiful grounds and small golf course. **$$$**
Tropical Lodge, at the eastern end of Malecón, tel: 809 538 2480. Good value, with pool and restaurant. **$**

San Pedro de Macorís
Howard Johnson Hotel Macoríx, Malecón, tel: 809 529 2100. Pool, good service and pleasant atmosphere. **$$**

Santiago de los Caballeros
Aloha Sol, Calle del Sol 150, tel: 809 583 0090. Chic and pleasant; quiet, though right in the middle of town. **$$**
Hotel Gran Almirante, Avenida Estrella Sadhalá 10, Los Jardines, tel: 809 580 1992. Casino and Spanish restaurant for business clientele. **$$**
Matum, Las Carreras 1, tel: 809 581 3107. Traditional, renovated hotel, near the noisy Parque Monumento. **$$**

Santo Domingo
Aída, El Conde 464 with Espaillat, tel: 809 685 7692. Family-run budget accommodation in the heart of the old city. Popular; the best rooms have a balcony overlooking the stylish shops. Unfortunately the interior rooms have no windows but they do have air conditioning. **$**

Antiguo Hotel Europa, Arzobispo Meriño, tel: 809 285 0005. Lovely early 20th-century building with iron balconies and tiled floors. Renovated rooms and suites. **$$**

El Beaterio, Duarte 8, tel: 809 687 8657. Sixteenth-century guesthouse with rooms set around a courtyard, lovely patio garden and roof terrace. Antique furniture inside. **$**

Conde de Peñalba, El Conde on the corner of Parque Colón, tel: 809 688 7121. Central location in the colonial zone, with a variety of rooms. The best have a balcony overlooking the square and the city's cathedral. The restaurant downstairs opens onto the square. **$$**

Courtyard by Marriott, Avenida Máximo Gómez 50-A, tel: 809 685 1010. Modern chain hotel located near the US Embassy and the theatre. Lots of amenities and services for the business traveller. **$$**

Duque de Wellington, Avenida Independencia 304, tel: 809 682 4525. Good budget option, with 28 basic rooms; TV and fridge. Bar and restaurant on site. **$**

Francés, Calle Las Mercedes, corner Calle Arzobispo Meriño, tel: 809 685 9331. Small hotel in colonial building with lovely patio. **$$$**

Hostal Nicolás Nader, Calle Duarte, tel: 809 687 6674. Small and charming hotel in colonial centre. **$$$**

No vacancies

Most large beach resorts operate on an all-inclusive basis, taking block bookings from tour operators in the tourists' home countries. As a result, it is often difficult to find a room for a night or two by simply turning up. Sometimes, however, hotel managers are willing to offer a discounted room rate if the hotel is not full, especially out of season. It is always worth asking.

Jaragua, Avenida George Washington 367, tel: 809 221 2222. Deluxe hotel with excellent amenities for business travellers. **$$$**

Melía Santo Domingo, Avenida George Washington 365, tel: 809 221 6666. Luxury atmosphere with good business and sporting facilities. **$$$**

Nicolás de Ovando, Calle Las Damas 53 (Zona Colonial), tel: 809 685 9955. Former governor's house with lots of historic ambience. The property has been renovated and claims to be the most luxurious hotel in town. **$$$**

Palacio, Calle Duarte 106, tel: 809 682 4730. Spanish-colonial-style hotel, small and attractive with heavy wooden furniture. **$$**

Saint-Amad, Arzobispo Meriño 353, tel: 809 687 1447. A renovated colonial house with 14 rooms and a restaurant. **$$**

Villa Italia, Avenida Independencia 1107, tel: 809 682 3373. A good value budget option in a very central location. **$$**

Sosúa

Sea Horse Ranch, 2km (1 mile) east of town, tel: 809 571 3880. Villas with private beach and horse riding facilities. **$$$**

PierGiorgio Palace Hotel, la Puntilla 1, tel: 809 571 2626. Italian-owned, with Victorian décor and great sea views. **$$**

Casa Marina Beach Club, tel: 809 571 3690. All-inclusive resort with a large swimming pool and a full range of facilities. **$$**

Playa Chiquita Beach Resort, tel: 809 571 2800. Out of town place with beach. **$$**

On the Waterfront, Dr. Rosen 1, El Batey, tel: 809 571 3024. On cliff with sea views, cabins and pool. **$**

Tropix, tel: 809 571 2291. Small and inexpensive, but with pleasant grounds and a swimming pool. **$**

INDEX